WAUGH IN ABYSSINIA

Books by Evelyn Waugh

PRB: An Essay on the Pre-Raphaelite Brotherhood (1926, 1982)
Rossetti: His Life and Works (1928)
Decline and Fall (1928)
Vile Bodies (1930)
Labels (1930)
Remote People (1931)
Black Mischief (1932)
A Handful of Dust (1934)
Ninety-Two Days (1934)
Edmund Campion (1935)
Mr Loveday's Little Outing and Other Sad Stories (1936)
Waugh in Abyssinia (1936)
Scoop (1938)
Robbery Under Law (1939)
Put Out More Flags (1942)
Work Suspended (1942)
Brideshead Revisited (1945)
When the Going was Good (1946)
Scott-King's Modern Europe (1947)
Wine in Peace and War (1947)
The Loved One (1948)
Work Suspended and Other Stories (1949)
Helena (1950)
The Holy Places (1952)
Men at Arms (1952)
Love Among the Ruins (1953)
Officers and Gentlemen (1955)
The Ordeal of Gilbert Pinfold (1957)
The Life of the Right Reverend Ronald Knox (1959)
A Tourist in Africa (1960)
Unconditional Surrender (1961)
Basil Seal Rides Again (1963)
A Little Learning (1964)
Essays, Articles and Reviews (1984)

WAUGH IN ABYSSINIA

Evelyn Waugh

METHUEN

First published in Great Britain 1936
by Longmans, Green & Co Ltd
This edition published 1984
by Methuen London Ltd
11 New Fetter Lane, London EC4P 4EE
Printed and bound in Great Britain
by Richard Clay (The Chaucer Press) Ltd
Bungay, Suffolk

British Library Cataloguing in Publication Data

Waugh, Evelyn
  Waugh in Abyssinia.
  1. Italo-Ethiopian War, 1935–1936 –
  Personal narratives
  I. Title
  963'.056'0924   DT387.8

  ISBN 0–413–54830–9

FOR

KITTY & PERRY

WHO, I HAVE NO DOUBT, WILL AFFECT TO
RECOGNISE THINLY DISGUISED AND RATHER
FLATTERING PORTRAITS OF THEMSELVES
IN THIS NARRATIVE;

WITH MY LOVE

CONTENTS

NOTE

This morning, after the final proofs of the first chapter had gone to press, there have appeared in the English newspapers some notices of Marshal de Bono's book on the war. I have not seen the book. The notices consist of a few quotations isolated from their context, interspersed in a highly tendentious commentary, and surmounted by sensational headlines. They may well prove misleading. At the moment I see no reason to alter any of the conclusions reached in this chapter.

E. W.

OCTOBER 9TH, 1936.

I

THE INTELLIGENT WOMAN'S GUIDE TO THE
ETHIOPIAN QUESTION

I

"Although the benefits of a civilised Protectorate are very evident, it is, I confess, with a feeling almost of sadness that I reflect that since I said farewell to Johannis at Afgol, on December 16, 1887, no other European can ever grasp the hand of an Independent Emperor of Ethiopia."

These words, published in 1892 in Mr. Gerald Portal's account [1] of his embassy to Abyssinia—an undertaking, like most others in that country, accomplished only at the expense of acute privation and some danger, embarrassed by the treachery of native guides and the ceremonious discourtesies of native noblemen; like most others, fruitless of result—record what an informed and, on the whole, sympathetic observer in the last century foresaw as the inevitable development of Ethiopian history.

He was writing at the close of a decade which had

[1] *My Mission to Abyssinia*, by Gerald H. Portal, C.B. (1892).

been marked by sensational changes in the constitution of Africa; changes still active whose only logical outcome was the division and occupation of the entire continent by the people of Europe. In the previous decade Livingstone and Stanley had made their momentous journeys across hitherto totally unknown country. Livingstone had inspired a resurgence of missionary spirit comparable, though in many respects dissimilar, to that of the sixteenth century—Catholics, Lutherans, Anglicans, Baptists had followed the laborious stages of his great journey, eager to reclaim the Africans from slavery and superstition. Stanley appealed more particularly to the commercial ambitions of his age. The industrial revolution, which had begun by giving more wealth to nearly everybody, had reached its second stage in which enormous, yearly increasing accumulations of surplus capital were falling into a small, yearly diminishing number of hands; the need of the time was for new sources of raw material, new markets, but, more than anything, for new fields of profitable investment. It was in his private capacity as a capitalist that Stanley's patron, King Leopold of Belgium, founded the International African Association. But in the 'eighties the exploitation of Africa took on a national and political complexion. France in the arduous years that followed the Prussian war saw a possibility of recovering in Africa the prestige she had lost in Europe. England, concerned primarily with safeguarding the route to India, possessed of ample territories in the temperate zones for the settlement of her surplus population, at first hung back, repeatedly and explicitly discouraging expansion of her coastal trading stations, until forced into competition by Germany.

It was not until 1884 that Bismarck disclosed his ambitions of African Empire; from the moment that he did so he became the dominating engineer of the partition. Africa was enormous; there was room for everyone; its wealth was illimitable; there, looming preternaturally large in the mists of legend and travellers' tales, lay the solution that Europe was seeking; there the ambitions and energies that with disastrous regularity rose to threaten the progress of civilisation, might have full and harmless scope. His concern, while obtaining all for his own people which generations might require, was that the frictions aroused in the scramble should not imperil the settlement of Europe so recently and satisfactorily achieved. The Congress of Berlin met in the winter of 1884 and the Powers discussed their claims and intentions. All were agreed upon the basic assumption: Africa was open to partition; any part of it that was held only by its own natives was a no-man's-land which any European might claim. Boundaries were to be on a strictly national basis [1]; it only remained to define the rules by which they should be drawn.

---

[1] The Congo Free State was brought into being, but from the first was mainly and soon exclusively Belgian.

Ten years earlier, when European interest was limited to a fringe of coastal trading stations, it had been vaguely held that, as mineral rights are prolonged from the earth's surface to its centre, the hinterland of these stations was legitimately theirs for an indefinite depth, if and when expansion should seem desirable. Such a theory was clearly applicable only to a circular and perfectly homogeneous continent; it had, moreover, the grave objection that considerable strips of the African coast were claimed on historic grounds by weak and, it was believed, retrograde states such as Portugal and Zanzibar. At Berlin an attempt was made to define what constituted ' effective occupation ' and ' spheres of influence.' In practice, however, boundaries continued to be marked by the process of local adventure by explorers and leisurely adjustment in their respective Chanceries.

The most remarkable feature of the partition was the speed with which it was accomplished. In less than ten years the whole of pagan Africa was in the hands of one or other of the European Powers. Explorers pushed on from village to village armed with satchels of draft treaties upon which hospitable chiefs were induced to set their mark; native interpreters made gibberish of the legal phraseology; inalienable tribal rights were exchanged for opera hats and musical boxes; some potentates, such as the Sultan of Sokoto, thought they were accepting tribute when they were receiving a subsidy in lieu of their sovereign rights,[1] others that it was the white man's polite custom to collect souvenirs of this kind; if, when they found they had been tricked, they resisted the invaders, they were suppressed with the use of the latest lethal machinery: diplomats in Europe drew frontiers across tracts of land of which they were totally ignorant, negligently overruling historic divisions of race and culture and the natural features of physical geography, consigning to the care of one or other white race millions of men who had never seen a white face. A task which was to determine the future history of an entire continent, requiring the highest possible degrees of scholarship and statesmanship, was rushed through in less than ten years.

But the avarice, treachery, hypocrisy and brutality of the partition are now a commonplace which needs no particularisation. Indeed the popular view is to exaggerate the criminality; to accept the fact as something inexcusable but irreparable; a great wrong, never to be repeated, committed in another, more barbarous age. It is worth remembering, at the present crisis, how lately these things were done and also how many of the high qualities of European civilisation appeared in the process. In the lowest category, the financiers who stayed in Europe at their offices were men of daring; what they risked was a small thing but it was what they valued most

[1] *The Dual Mandate in British Tropical Africa*, by Lord Lugard (1922).

highly; orthodox big-business distrusted the travellers' tales of African wealth; it was a gamble in which fortunes were lost as well as won. The explorers were doing what no men had done before them; they did not travel at the head of an army but in small companies, often alone, in unknown dangers. Many lost their lives, almost all lost their health, and of the mixed motives which impelled them— adventure, patriotism, science—avarice was usually the least important and the least rewarded. There were the administrators, who, for small salaries, brought justice and order into wicked places, and, in the highest category of all, priests and nuns, missionaries of every sect and doctors, whose whole lives were an atonement for the crimes of their countrymen. It is worth remembering that these achievements were not exclusively or even predominantly British.

It is worth remembering indeed, in the present circumstances, the particular nature of the reproach which attaches to England. France, Germany and Belgium were the more ruthless; we the more treacherous. We went into the shady business with pious expressions of principle; we betrayed the Portuguese and the Sultan of Zanzibar,[1] renouncing explicit and freshly made guarantees of their territory; we betrayed Lobenguela and other native rulers in precisely the same method but with louder protestations of benevolent intention than our competitors;

[1] *The Partition of Africa*, by J. Scott Keltie (1893).

no matter into what caprice of policy our electorate chose to lead us, we preached on blandly and continuously; it was a trait which the world found difficult to tolerate; but we are still preaching.

2

In 1930 many Europeans exercised the privilege of grasping the hand of an Independent Emperor of Abyssinia.

On November 2 of that year Ras Tafari Makonnen was crowned King of Kings, Lion of Judah, Emperor Haile Selassie I at Addis Ababa. Delegations from the entire civilised world were present to wish him, in the name of their countries, a long and prosperous reign and to assure him of their friendly intentions. The Duke of Gloucester, attended by the Governors of the surrounding territories, represented Great Britain; the Prince of Udine, Italy; Marshal d'Esperey, France. Not only these great neighbouring Powers, but states as remote in their interests as Holland and Poland chose to interpret the announcement of the succession as an invitation; everyone was eager to observe this unique monarchy which had defied all predictions and retained its independence. Abyssinian hospitality was strained almost unendurably in their accommodation. It was widely believed among the populace that these braided figures had come to pay homage.

The new Emperor was treated to every mark

of independent royalty. Press photographers and cinema men jostled before him, divesting the prolix solemnities of almost all their decency. Presents of biblical diversity were heaped upon him—hock from Germany, statuary from Greece, bedroom furniture from Egypt. Distant editors were demanding stories of ' barbaric splendour ' and, while earnest palace officials were trying to interest the visiting correspondents in the new programme of administrative reform and social service, the cable office was glutted with press messages describing the rough and often shoddy pageantry in terms that would have been barely applicable to the court of Suleiman the Magnificent or of the Mogul Emperors of India.

Except at the military reviews the Abyssinians were not conspicuous. At the coronation itself only a few dozen were present—the great Rases, who sat among the delegations on the dais, gorgeous, rather morose personages in comic gild coronets, and a handful of smaller chiefs who had fought their way past the royal guards and now dozed fitfully on the floor in far corners of the pavilion. Besides these, the European visitors were aware of the existence, at a great distance, of a dense, half-human rabble that was constantly held at bay by the police; a mass of curly black heads that were for ever being whacked with staves; a great tide of grubby white garments which flowed into the city at dawn from the surrounding hillside and ebbed out at nightfall, assisted in all its motions by unremitting direction from canes and rifle butts.

The focal point, the still hub of all the turmoil, was Tafari himself; a small, elegant figure, Oriental rather than African, formal, circumspect, inscrutable; he moved like a vested statue carried in a religious procession; he sat upright and impassive among the sprawling and fidgeting European delegates; it scarcely seemed possible that anyone could take pleasures as sadly as he took those of his European guests; at the racecourse he spoke to no one, but sat under his canopy, motionless except for a slight inclination in acknowledgment of the salutes of the winning riders; in the ballroom he sat by the wall, his tiny, polished shoes just clear of the dancers.

That crowded week was the consummation of months of feverish activity, years of quiet plotting. A few days earlier he had been driving about the city, directing in person the planting of the flag-staffs, the erection of triumphal arches; he had discussed every detail of the extravagant entertainment. He was able, now, to sit and enjoy his triumph. For years he had been playing a delicate game between the Powers and his own people; abroad and to foreign visitors he had shown himself as the descendant of a historic line of Christian kings and queens, representative of an ancient civilisation, a statesman who would distil all that was most valuable in the modern world, the friend of missionaries, doctors and schoolmasters; he had explained his country as a mediæval state, a cohesive whole held together by the intricate bonds of feudalism, its occasional disorders as those which had beset Europe seven centuries ago—the over-mighty subject, a too dominant clergy. At home he had presented himself as the man who understood the ways of the foreigner, to whom his people must surrender their ancient rights of local independence if they were to retain any independence at all. He could make no pre-eminent claim to authority on grounds of heredity; the real Emperor was in chains, few people knew where. Tafari was the man chosen for a job; one of many great noblemen elected by the others, one of themselves, set the task for which they knew he was suited, to continue the tortuous, dangerous policy that had so far succeeded, of playing off the Powers against each other. It was thus that Abyssinia, contrary to all reasonable prediction, had survived so far, not only intact but enormously augmented.

But in Tafari's mind—pathetically compounded of primitive simplicity and primitive suspicion, of the traditional Christian righteousness, that had found occasional expression even in characters as intemperate as the Emperor Theodore's, and traditional savage hostility to European standards—there was a belief, half formed, never fully operative, that there had lately been a change in the constitution of the world. Abyssinia had survived through the rivalries of the Powers; now these rivalries were at an end; old wrongs had been forgotten, the map had finally been drawn, rolled up, sealed, at Versailles and Geneva. The Powers still maintained their mission to rule Africa; they had consecrated it in the phrase of the League Covenant : "*The well being and development of peoples not yet able to stand by themselves under the strenuous conditions of the modern world form a sacred trust of civilisation . . . best entrusted to advanced nations.*" Germany, by her defeat in battle, was held to have proved herself unworthy of this trust and her share was redistributed, great parts being given to the Boers—with the single exception of the Abyssinians the most notoriously oppressive admini-strators of subject peoples in Africa.[1] But Abyssinia remained unappropriated. More than that, through the good offices of her old enemies the Italians, she had inexplicably—miraculously, it might well appear to a people as confident of Divine favour as the Abyssinians—stepped into place beside the con-querors. She was a member of the League of Nations, admitted on equal terms to the councils of the world, her territory guaranteed absolutely and explicitly; that vast and obscure agglomeration of feudal fiefs, occupied military provinces, tributary sultanates, trackless no-man's-lands roamed by homi-cidal nomads; undefined in extent, unmapped,

[1] The massacre by air bombing of the Bondelzwarts, a primitive race in ex-German South-West Africa, by the South African mandatory government, on the grounds that "they could not or would not pay a tax on their dogs," was mentioned at Geneva in 1923, but resulted in no reproof or compensation.

unexplored, in part left without law, in part grossly subjugated; the brightly coloured patch in the schoolroom atlas marked, for want of a more exact system of terminology, 'Ethiopian Empire,' had been recognised as a single state whose integrity was the concern of the world. Tafari's own new dynasty had been accepted by the busy democracies as the government of this area; his enemies were their enemies; there would be money lent him to arm against rebels, experts to advise him; when trouble was brewing he would swoop down from the sky and take his opponents unawares; the fabulous glories of Prester John were to be reincarnate; roads, telephones, tractors, chemical manures, clinics, colleges and new hygienic gaols.

Forty years of confused history, in Africa and Europe, lay between Tafari and Johannis. It was during this period that the Ethiopian Empire came into existence.

3

At the beginning of the nineteenth century Abyssinia consisted of the four mountain kingdoms of Amhara, Shoa, Tigre and Gojjam, situated in almost complete isolation from outside intercourse; their neighbours were hostile pagans and Mohammedans of negro and Hamitic race; the Abyssinians [1] were

[1] The name, a corruption of the Arabic Habasha, is variously derived as meaning 'Mongrels' and as 'members of the Arabian Habashat tribe.' Hamitic and Semitic have now little precise

Christians of mixed Semitic and Hamitic blood; they believed they had migrated from Arabia at some unrecorded date, probably before the Christian era; they employed a common literary language, Ghiz, which had some affinity with ancient Armenian, and spoke dialects derived from it, Tigrean and Amharic; they shared a common culture and feudal organisation and recognised a paramount King of Kings as their nominal head; from time to time in their history the King of Kings had asserted effective government and extended his rule to the outlying tribes; in the century before Mohammed he had controlled a great part of the Red Sea coast and the Yemen; there are ancient traditions of a golden age in which he had ruled from Khartoum to Nyassa, but by 1818, when, it is thought, Kassa was born, the office had become purely titular, shared often by several claimants at once, and the four kingdoms were practically autonomous; they were at constant war against one another, against their neighbours, and against internal rebels. Kassa was the son of a minor Amhara chief; his mother lived by selling *kosso*, a specific against tapeworm, in the streets of Gondar; like most Abyssinians with any claim to gentle birth he traced his descent from Solomon and the Queen of Sheba. From living by brigandage in the low countries, Kassa succeeded in making himself King

meaning. Professor Kolmodin of Upsala denies that Abyssinians originated from Arabia. Malaya and Oceania have been suggested as their source.

13

of Kings, under the name of Theodore, and for the first time in centuries established a central monarchy over the whole country; in later life he became an alcoholic and in his cups imprisoned at Magdala a handful of European adventurers, including two who had been given British consular privileges. In 1867 an expedition was sent to rescue them under Lord Napier, and next year, at the cost of £9,000,000, was successful. Theodore committed suicide at the moment of defeat and the British troops left the country to another period of chaos. In 1872 the Ras of Tigre became King of Kings under the name of John (the Johannis whose independent hand was grasped by Mr Gerald Portal). He was much pestered during his short reign by European bagmen and died, very gloriously, at the moment of victory over the Dervishes. His reign is notable as marking the beginning of the struggle for empire between the Italians and the Abyssinians which resulted in the wars of 1895 and 1935. The nature of this struggle has never been widely understood in Europe.

The Italians first established themselves in the Red Sea by the purchase—by a private trading company which was later absorbed by the state—of the small port of Assab on the edge of the Danakil country. In 1885, at the invitation of the British, they settled further west at Massawa. The collapse of Turkish-Egyptian power before the Mahdi was promising a redistribution in this part of Africa (it had the double effect of laying open to occupation a number of important towns both on the coast and in the interior and at the same time leaving an extremely dangerous neighbour in the Soudan; the pressure on the flank of both parties by the Mahdists must be taken into account throughout the succeeding years). We had temporarily used Massawa to assist the evacuation of the Soudan garrisons; it was a place of few attractions, troublesome and expensive to maintain, but in the existing condition of competitive expansion it was certain that our evacuation would immediately result in its occupation by another Power; always anxious for the safety of our route to India, we preferred that it should fall to a small and friendly state, rather than to France. Accordingly we persuaded the Italians to take on our responsibility, pointing out that though the town itself was far from desirable it offered a fine starting-point for the exploitation of the interior. From then, for fifty years, our policy was to encourage Italian penetration in Abyssinia.

The hinterland between Massawa and Tigre was at that time one of the most insecure districts in Africa and Italian progress met with some reverses, the worst of which was the massacre at Dogeli of a part-military part-scientific exploring expedition of 500 men by an ambush of 20,000 Tigreans; but at Johannis's death in 1889 Abyssinia again seemed to disintegrate and offer an opportunity for Italian intervention of the kind that was proving successful all over Africa.

The mismanagement of this opportunity has been fully examined from every point of view.[1] The radical causes were indecision and false economy by the parliamentary government in Rome, undue and ignorant interference with the men on the spot, contradictory policy pursued by the men on the spot due largely to the difficulties of communication between the Italians treating with Menelik and those treating with Mangasha, a fatal but very natural underestimation of the abilities of Menelik, and a less excusable failure to realise the basic unity that lay below the superficial antagonisms of the Abyssinian rulers.

Johannis had acknowledged two successors, Menelik, Ras of Shoa, and Mangasha of the Tigre, his illegitimate son, both of whom commanded a very powerful following. Menelik was little known in the north, but while Johannis was busy with the Dervishes and the Italians he had been making sensational conquests in the non-Abyssinian countries in the west and south, among the Kaffa and Galla peoples, the most important of which was the Emirate of Harar, an ancient, wealthy and cultured Arab city state, recently evacuated by its Egyptian garrison, over which he put his nephew Ras Makonnen. From then onwards Harar suffered from direct Abyssinian rule more continuously and acutely than any part of the empire. Menelik, in these expeditions, was

[1] Perhaps the best source for the English reader is *The Campaign of Adowa and the Rise of Menelik*, by G. F.-H. Berkeley (1902).

furnished with arms and advice by a number of more or less shady Europeans, the majority of whom were French; his soldiers were better equipped and better organised than any in Africa. Any enemy of his could count on support from his Mohammedan neighbours, in particular from the powerful Sultan of Aussa and the Somalis of the Ogaden.

Mangasha had the prestige which still surrounded the historic north, the sacred city of Axum, the original home of the Abyssinian people; he had moreover the loyalty—about the only unqualified loyalty discernible in the whole affair—of the great warrior Ras Alula, who, immediately on Johannis's death, drove out Menelik's agent Seyoum. The factions were thus, apparently, equally matched and Italian policy alternated disastrously between the two; their forces meanwhile pushed forward and occupied what, in 1935, constituted the Italian colony of Eritrea, including large sectors of purely Abyssinian highland. When Baldissera, the leader of this advance, resigned, the Italian party in favour of a Shoan alliance was left supreme. Accordingly two treaties were concluded with Menelik, acknowledging his position as Emperor, establishing a protectorate of his dominions, and fixing a frontier between it and the Italian colony. This situation was accepted by the European Powers, and when in December 1889 Menelik announced his accession, he was informed by Great Britain and Germany that he had acted improperly in addressing himself to them directly instead of through the Italian government. In March 1890 Abyssinia was represented by Italy at the second Congress of Brussels. Atlases of the period mark an area broken only by the French 'Protectorate of Tajurra' (French Somaliland) and an indefinite British strip on the south coast of the Gulf of Aden, as 'Italian Abyssinia.' The matter, however, was far from being settled. There were ambiguities in the Amharic version of the treaty of Ucciali, of which Menelik quickly took advantage. Count Antonelli, who had arranged it, hurried back to Shoa. Negotiations were resumed with all the cumbrous machinery of the Abyssinian court—the prevarications and evasions, the diplomatic illnesses, the endless exchanges of irrelevant compliments, the lethargy and cunning of which Menelik was a master. At length it was agreed that he should accept a protectorate for five years and the Italians should give up some of the ground they had won in Tigre. The matter was settled and signed; Antonelli examined the document with his interpreter and discovered that its provisions were exactly contrary to what had been decided—a complete renunciation by Italy of all rights in Abyssinia. Menelik regretted that there had been a misunderstanding but refused to reopen the matter. It was a trick that would have been childish enough, were it not backed by a daily increasing armed strength. Still the Roman government could not decide on resolute action. Negotiations were begun through other channels.

Finally, in February 1893, in a supremely ill-considered attempt at conciliation, the Italians made Menelik a present of a huge consignment of cartridges. He at once formally denounced the treaty of Ucciali. He had got all he wanted. A month later he sent a declaration to the Powers asserting his independence and defining his frontiers so that they included two provinces under Italian administration and vast tracts of neighbouring country where his troops had not hitherto set foot. The Italians had not only armed their enemy but they had antagonised their remaining allies. The caravan of ammunition had proceeded slowly from Harar, attracting a maximum of attention. All over the Aussa and the Ogaden it was known that the Italians were betraying them; from Tigre Mangasha came to make his submission. Four years before the Tigreans had refused Menelik entrance to Axum for his coronation; now they allowed him to introduce men of his own into all their commands. He could contemplate war without misapprehension.

Nothing can be further from historical fact than to picture Menelik as a black Bruce, recklessly defying a powerful invader. He had calculated his chances and his opportunities astutely. He was well informed about the relative strengths of the European Powers. He was no savage chief to whom any white face was a divine or diabolic portent. He knew that the Italians were a poor people, with no recent military tradition; their government was hampered by the ineptitude in handling parliamentary forms consistently shown by the Mediterranean peoples. The British had spent £9,000,000 on their expedition against Theodore; Rome now reluctantly voted £750,000. Menelik knew that if the British met with a reverse, as they had at Khartoum, they would draw on their limitless reserves and, in their own time, return in overwhelming strength; if the Italians failed, they would fail decisively.

The defeat, in the spring of 1896, *was* decisive but far from ignominious; at the opening of the campaign Baratieri fought a masterly action against the Dervishes, while Tosselli subdued the Tigre in three days. In 1895 the Italians held the line Adowa-Makale-Adigrat and in 1896 had an advance post at Amba Alagi. Then Menelik arrived in the north in overpowering strength; his speed of mobilisation had been beyond the calculations of European strategists; until the last disastrous days the Italians were completely unaware of the numbers that were coming against them; each man carrying his own rations and ammunition, trotting indefatigably along the mountain tracks from all corners of the four kingdoms, a force of 100,000 men had silently assembled. Up to the last moment, even after the Italian retreat had begun, Ras Makonnen, the father of Haile Selassie, was flirting with Italian proposals to desert; finally he threw himself, with the Harar garrison, on to Menelik's side. At Adowa, on March 1, Baratieri's army was annihilated by a well-equipped force outnumbering it by eight to one.

During the preceding retreat and in the hopeless final engagement acts of courage on the part of the Italian officers and of fidelity on the part of the native troops were performed which would have lent glory to any army. Nearly 1000 white troops were killed and 4000 or 3000 askaris; few wounded survived; the white prisoners who wer to Menelik himself were well treated and released.[1]

Glutted with victory, Menelik's army disperse and he was unable to follow up his the Italians rallied, defeated the Derv conquered Kasala and checked the Abyssini at Tukruf, while another force moved to of Adigrat. Till then Menelik had hope Tigre of the invaders; he now came to te boundary was drawn, which remained in force until October 1935, leaving a substantial corner of Abyssinia within the colony of Eritrea. In return Italy withdrew all claims to a protectorate.

In the twelve years which followed Menelik created the Ethiopian Empire.[2] The process was

---

[1] In an attempt to minimise the savagery of the victorious army, it is claimed that only thirty white prisoners were castrated. The truth is that only thirty survived and returned to Rome ; innumerable others were reckoned among those killed in action; a few are said to have lived but to have preferred, in shame, to remain in Africa.

[2] In the following pages ' Abyssinian ' will be used to qualify the Amharic-speaking, Semitic, Christian peoples of the four mountain kingdoms ; ' Ethiopian ' the tribes and naturalised immigrants (of whom there were a considerable number) subject to their rule.

closely derived from the European model; sometimes the invaded areas were overawed by the show of superior force and accepted treaties of protection; sometimes they resisted and were slaughtered with the use of the modern weapons which were being imported both openly and illicitly in enormous numbers; sometimes they were simply recorded as Ethiopian without their own knowledge. The history of the reign becomes a monotonous succession of the place names of conquered territories. Already, before the Italian war, Menelik had taken possession of huge Galla and Guraghi territories to the southwest of Shoa. In 1897 he sent an expedition into Kaffa, captured the king, and absorbed the country. In 1898 Makonnen defeated and secured the nominal allegiance of the Somali tribes of the Ogaden. In the same year a Frenchman in Menelik's employ, Léon Danegon, returned to Addis Ababa after a triumphal expedition at the head of 15,000 Abyssinian soldiers, which had penetrated nearly to the shores of Lake Rudolf; he presented Menelik with an itinerary specifying the tribes and villages visited, all of which were promptly declared Ethiopian territory. A similar expedition, twice as strong, led by a Russian, had been sent out the previous year; it now returned to report the submission of the kings and peoples of Ghimirra. Kadaret, Kallabat, Fazogli were captured by his nephew Tasama, accompanied by French, Swiss, and Russian advisers, and the Ethiopian flag was planted on the banks of the White

Nile. In 1899 Borana, a long strip of lowland on the Soudanese border, Beni Shangul, Gunza and Gubba, were conquered, and a second attempt was made on the Ogaden, where 9000 Somalis were killed in a battle south of Jijiga. In 1900 there were further submissions by the Nilotic peoples north of Lake Rudolf; a campaign was launched against the Aussa, who did not submit until 1909, at the same time as the Sultanates of Teru and Biru. During this period there were three formidable risings in Tigre; Gojjam was put under Shoan rule in 1901 after its king had been poisoned. In 1903 there was another campaign against the Ogaden.[1] In 1913 Menelik died after having spent his later years in a partially comatose condition; he left his country with nominal dominion over an area three or four times its size, inhabited by a complex variety of peoples all totally dissimilar to it in religion, language, race and history.

It is impossible to give any general survey of the government of the subject provinces; material is scanty and conditions varied so radically from place to place that the observations of no particular traveller can be accepted as having any universal application. In general it may be said that, with the exception of the Hararis, the Mohammedan peoples came off the most lightly; the Sultan of Jimma retained virtual independence until 1933; the Danakils, Aussa and Somalis were left in their savage

[1] *A History of Ethiopia*, by Sir E. A. Wallis Budge (1928).

condition, unworried except by the occasional visits of Imperial tax-gatherers—an event which had more the complexion of a raid by brigands than an administrative act. The pagan peoples of the south and west were treated with wanton brutality unequalled even in the Belgian Congo. Some areas were depopulated by slavers; in others Abyssinian garrisons were permanently quartered on the people, whose duty it was to support them and their descendants. Abyssinian officials, with retinues which varied in size from a royal guard to a standing army, lived upon the work and taxes of the original inhabitants; their function was not to protect but to hold in subjection; fighting was the only occupation they recognised. It was not a question of a tolerable system being subject to abuse, but of an intolerable system. When, in the days of the mobilisation, reports appeared in Europe of the movements of 'the army of Kambata' or 'the army of Sidamo,' an impression was given of national solidarity that was entirely fictitious. If the subject peoples were willing to fight for the Abyssinians, it was argued, their rule could not be as oppressive as the Italians pretended. In fact these provincial armies were the Abyssinian garrisons recalled for service, as British forces might be withdrawn from Egypt or Palestine; their very number, swarming past the Emperor, hour after hour, capering and boasting on their way to the front, testified to the dead weight of the Abyssinian occupation.

Here was imperialism devoid of a single redeeming element. However sordid the motives and however gross the means by which the white races established —and are still establishing—themselves in Africa, the result has been, in the main, beneficial, for there are more good men than bad in Europe and there is a predisposition towards justice and charity in European culture ; a bias, so that it cannot for long run free without inclining to good; things which began wickedly have turned out well. The very feature which to-day seems most odious in the original depredations—the unctuous avowals of high principle with which they were made—has itself provided a check. The significance of the Congo atrocities is not so much that they were committed as that they were exposed and suppressed; there is a conscience in Europe which, when informed and aroused, is more powerful than any vested interest. Even in the terms of nineteenth-century liberalism there has been more gain than loss to the African natives. It was to the interest of the exploiters to preserve the exploited from the endemic ravages of plague, famine and massacre to which they were heirs, to educate them for profitable contacts with an advanced machinery of commerce and administration; waste lands have been made fertile, hunted peoples have been made secure, vile little tyrannies have been abolished. The Abyssinians had nothing to give their subject peoples, nothing to teach them. They brought no crafts or knowledge, no new system of agriculture, drainage or roadmaking, no medicine or hygiene, no higher political organisation, no superiority except in their magazine rifles and belts of cartridges. They built nothing; they squatted in the villages in the thatched huts of the conquered people, dirty, idle and domineering, burning the timber, devouring the crops, taxing the meagre stream of commerce that seeped in from outside, enslaving the people. It was not, as in the early days of the Belgian Congo, that bad men with too much power, too far from supervision, were yielding to appetites of which their own people denied them satisfaction. The Abyssinians imposed what was, by its nature, a deadly and hopeless system. In the tin-roofed offices at Addis Ababa the *Jeunesse d'Ethiopie* [1] drew up occasional programmes of reform; there was a model province at Asfa Tafari conveniently near the railway line to allow visiting Europeans a cursory inspection; palace officials were always ready to explain in glib French how, bit by bit, the whole Empire was to be brought under a new and enlightened system—these things affected the nation as little as might a committee of women welfare workers in Europe passing a resolution deploring the use of tobacco. Even in the *Jeunesse d'Ethiopie* itself there was little real desire for change; a weekly visit to the cinema, a preference for whisky over *tedj*, toothbrush moustaches in place of the traditional and imposing beards, patent leather

[1] The society of ' progressive ' Abyssinians.

shoes and a passable dexterity with fork and spoon
were the Western innovations that these young men
relished; these, and a safe climb to eminence behind
the broad, oxlike backs of the hereditary aristocracy.
Perhaps the Emperor himself thought of something
more ambitious; perhaps a handful of his circle
vaguely shared his thoughts; but the governing class
as a whole were immovable. Something, it was
realised, had to be done to ensure the support of the
mysterious, remote, incalculably powerful organisation at Geneva, of which Abyssinia had become a
part, something on paper, neatly typewritten in
French and English. Tricking the European was a
national craft; evading issues, promising without
the intention of fulfilment, tricking the paid foreign
advisers, tricking the legations, tricking the visiting
international committees—these were the ways by
which Abyssinia had survived and prospered.

It was generally supposed among her neighbours
that Ethiopia would disintegrate at the death of
Menelik, and in provision for this they made an agreement in 1906 renouncing competitive action in the
subsequent resettlement. France and England had
no desire for extensive additions of territory, con-
tenting themselves with a guarantee of their interests
in the railway zone and the Blue Nile respectively.
(England, as was shown in the judiciously revealed
Maffey report, has not changed her ambitions since.)
The principle of 1891 was reaffirmed that the greater

27

part of Ethiopia lay within Italy's legitimate sphere of influence. In an exchange of notes between the British and Italian governments in December 1925 the understanding was made more explicit; Great Britain undertook to support the constantly evaded Italian request to build a railway through Western Ethiopia connecting her two colonies, recognised an exclusive Italian economic influence in West Abyssinia and the whole territory to be crossed by the railway, and promised to support all Italian demands for concessions in that territory. There was complete agreement between all parties. If Ethiopia broke up, Italy was to assume whatever political authority she desired; if it remained intact she was to develop it by means of peaceful economic penetration.

Ethiopia did not break up on Menelik's death. There were grave disorders, but government of a kind was maintained. The crisis did not come until the summer of 1916, when, at the height of the European war, no one could contemplate an expensive campaign in Africa. Lij Yasu, Menelik's successor, was deposed after a series of engagements and risings which continued sporadically until his death in 1935. He fell because he attempted to reorientate his empire. He was predominantly Mohammedan by blood (his father was a superficially Christianised Mohammedan chief; his mother, Menelik's daughter by a Mohammedan wife) and he conceived the idea of a vast East African Mohammedan state, under German-Turkish auspices, embracing the territories of the allied Powers. He tried to break the domination of the Abyssinians of the four Christian kingdoms and was broken by them. In the succeeding period the power was precariously shared between the Empress, the Shoan military party, represented by the veteran Fitaurari Hapta Giorgis, the Church represented by the Coptic Abuna—all strongly conservative—and Ras Tafari, the son of Ras Makonnen. It ended, not without bloodshed, in Tafari achieving supreme power.

At the peace conference, as is notorious, Italy received an inconsiderable fraction of the colonial advantages which had been promised her as the price of entering the war upon the side of the allied Powers, but she was in no mood for imperialistic adventures. The situation envisaged in the 1906 agreement had not fully come into being. Accordingly, she decided to encourage Abyssinian aspirations towards unity and reform, and with this end overcame British opposition and secured Abyssinia membership of the League of Nations. From then onwards her policy was an economic and cultural imperialism of the kind which the United States of America have imposed upon their unprogressive Latin neighbours and of which the Treaty of Friendship, signed in 1928, was intended to be the charter. It was the frustration of this policy which provoked the war of 1935.

In the spring and summer of 1935, while both sides were preparing for war and negotiations for peace were being made at Rome, Paris and Geneva in an atmosphere of increasing futility, the Italian Bureau of Propaganda issued a series of documents in English and French itemising the acts of offence perpetrated by the Abyssinians, which attracted little sympathy among the public to which they were addressed. The public utterances of Signor Mussolini had been rhetorical and uncompromising,[1] those of the Emperor of Abyssinia studiously temperate. The cinema-going public of Europe was accustomed to the spectacle of Signor Mussolini in exuberant baroque attitudes; of the Emperor hierarchic and remote as a figure from a Byzantine ikon; troops and war materials were daily being shipped from Italy to East Africa with the maximum of ostentation; the Abyssinians moved barefoot through unfrequented passes. For fifteen years the civilised world had been contemplating askance the destructive force of its scientific discoveries. In these circumstances complaints about Abyssinian ' aggression ' seemed patently absurd, and neither at Geneva nor in Europe at large were they seriously considered. ' Aggression ' was an unfortunate phrase, borrowed from the vocabulary of the League of Nations. There was never any positive intention among responsible Abyssinians to overrun the Italian colonies and add

[1] " Let no one hold any illusions in or out of Italy. We are tolerably circumspect before we make a decision, but once a decision is taken we march ahead and do not turn back . . . Better live as a lion one day than a hundred years as a sheep. . . . We must go forward until we achieve the Fascist Empire," etc.

them to the Ethiopian Empire; they talked of these things in their cups, but the Emperor, certainly, indulged in no fancies of that kind. There was, however, a firm determination to restrict to a minimum all intercourse between the two nations and to treat the Italians as the least rather than the most favoured of their three neighbours. They neither wanted Italy's friendship nor feared her enmity. Membership of the League of Nations corresponded exactly to the present of ammunition to Menelik in 1893; the Italians had armed Abyssinia against themselves; they had earned no recompense and no gratitude. Abyssinia had no further use for them. The days were past when a disorderly and undeveloped country needed to put herself under the particular protection of a great Power; what need had Abyssinia for Italian friendship when she had been given the friendship of the entire world ? This was the argument of the Court and *Jeunesse d'Ethiopie*, but in the huts of the soldiers and the tin-roofed palaces of the provincial governors it ran differently; it was thumped out on the oxhide war-drums and chanted by the minstrels, chuckled about over the horns of *tedj*; the Italians were the white men of Adowa; at every feast day throughout the country the veterans paraded in gala dress, rolling their eyes, whirling their swords, slavering at the mouth, stamping themselves into delirium as they re-enacted the slaughter of that day, yelling of the white blood they had shed. The Italians were

31

one with Kafa and the Shankalla, Guraghi and Galla, a conquered people, slaves. It was all very remote from the council chambers at Geneva, from the manifest accumulations of girders and wire and explosives on the quays of Massawa and Mogadishu, but it was the essential temper of the people which, refined and formalised, found its way into the official dealings of the Emperor and ministers.

The Italian complaints may be summarised as stating that Ethiopia was barbarous and zenophobic and that she had not fulfilled her engagements to Italy under the 1928 Treaty of Friendship. Of the truth of the first point there was never any serious doubt among informed people. Slavery and slave-raiding were universal; justice, when executed at all, was accompanied by torture and mutilation in a degree known nowhere else in the world; the central government was precarious and only rendered effective by repeated resort to armed force; disease was rampant. All were agreed upon the truth of these statements. The Covenant of the League assumed, and in some particulars specified, a cultural standard for its members to which Abyssinia nowhere approximated. The central government minimised, but admitted the existence of the problem. They contended that the solution lay within the country; in a generation Abyssinia would reform herself. There was no unanimity among foreign observers as to how much reliance could be placed on these assurances. In the absence of evidence most resorted to sentiment in forming their opinions. On the one side were the missionaries of all races and creeds. These were naturally disposed to credulity and charity. They preferred to believe the best of everyone; they were, moreover, bound to the Emperor by particular ties of gratitude: he gave them property and protection; some—one in particular who has been most eloquent in pleading the Ethiopian cause [1]—had taken the foolhardy step of assuming Ethiopian nationality ; the work they were doing was, in most cases, so patently altruistic that they encountered little hostility and some co-operation from their native superiors. Incongruously allied with these were the Europeans who deplored all European influence in Africa, and rejoiced to find an ' unspoiled ' area; who would have liked to preserve Ethiopia, in the way that national parks are isolated and preserved for animals, as a sanctuary for savages; extreme lovers of the picturesque who fostered lepers and eunuchs and brigand chiefs, as their milder brothers encouraged sulky yokels in England to perform folk dances on the village green. Added to these were a handful of travellers who had had the rare good fortune to be politely treated by the Abyssinians and were chivalrously disinclined to abuse the hospitality they had received. These were the elements which

[1] Immediately after the Italian occupation this man issued a retraction of his accusations. Although his original statements were given immense publicity in the English press, the retraction passed unnoticed.

constituted the pro-Abyssinian party until the great campaign of 1935 started, when the Socialists of Europe, in their hatred of the internal administration of Italy, nearly succeeded in precipitating world war in defence of an archaic African despotism.

The anti-Abyssinian party consisted of those who had done or attempted to do jobs in the country; it varied in composition from the consuls who were concerned in securing fulfilment of obligations towards their nationals and the cosmopolitan adventurers who had tried to trick the natives and found themselves tricked. These were convinced that there was no possibility of reform through the ordinary governmental channels and that European help would never be generally acceptable or effective as long as Abyssinia was an unconquered country. The zenophobia of the people was an insuperable barrier to all free co-operation. This is the feature of the country which has most impressed visiting writers—particularly the French. Djibouti has always been haunted by interested gossips who warn travellers of the dangers they will encounter up the line. Most people are disposed to settle high political questions in terms of the treatment they have received in casual encounters during their travels; a dishonest taxi-driver or an overbearing policeman embitter international relations more than the perfidy of governments. The English, on the whole, are intensely zenophobic, and for this reason their sympathies are most easily aroused on behalf

of nations with whom they have least acquaintance.
All of them know something about the French and
the Italians. They have been overcharged for their
luncheon in Paris; they have been made to walk on
the other side of the street in Rome. But only an
infinitesimal number have suffered the indignities of
travelling in Abyssinia. Those that have are inclined
to be intemperate about it.

The essence of the offence was that the Abyssinians,
in spite of being by any possible standard an inferior
race, persisted in behaving as superiors; it was not
that they were hostile, but contemptuous. The
white man, accustomed to other parts of Africa,
was disgusted to find the first-class carriages on the
railway usurped by local dignitaries; he found
himself subject to officials and villainous-looking men
at arms whose language he did not know, who
showed him no sort of preference on account of his
colour, and had not the smallest reluctance to using
force on him if he became truculent. There were,
of course, large tracts of Ethiopia where any
stranger, white or Abyssinian, was liable to be
murdered on sight. Few travellers penetrated to
those regions, and those who did were conscious
that they were doing something highly dangerous.
It was less glamorous to be in danger, as not in-
frequently happened, of being knocked down by
a policeman in the streets of the capital. The
Abyssinians were constantly coming to blows; any
direction of traffic was performed with buffeting

and whipping; an arrest invariably involved a fight; an evening's entertainment often resulted in the discharge of firearms, broken heads and chains for the whole party. It was the normal tenor of Abyssinian life, and Europeans, if they came to the country, were expected to share in it. Abyssinians rarely travelled, even within their own boundaries; the number who had been to Europe was minute. They judged Europeans as they saw them in Ethiopia, and what they saw did not impress them. The results aggravated the cause, for only Europeans negligent of their own dignity could maintain any relations with them. The Legations, anxious to preserve their own prestige, dissociated themselves as far as they could from their less reputable nationals; jealous of each other's influence they studiously avoided common action to support the rights that had been guaranteed to foreigners by treaties. The Abyssinians formed their opinion of Western civilisation from the deportment of journalists, press photographers and concession-hunters. The formidable dossier prepared by the Italians of outrages upon European dignity—partly acts of mob-hooliganism but chiefly of violence by the police—does not so much prove hostility as a sense of equality. They treated visitors rather better than their own people, but not so much better as to make the country agreeable.

Towards Europeans who wished to settle and make money in the country they adopted a less equitable manner. It was illegal for foreigners to own land in Ethiopia, but it was always possible to acquire by purchase temporary concessions for almost any kind of undertaking. The prospector had only to bribe his way into the presence of the responsible official, put down his deposit and lay his finger on any part of the map to receive permission to mine or farm there. It was when he arrived at the chosen place that his difficulties began; he would find his concession was already held under various titles by a dozen rival claimants, native and foreign; he would find labourers impossible to keep in decent discipline; he would find neighbours who pilfered and raided, against whom he could obtain no redress; he would find local officials who evinced scant regard for the documents he had obtained at Addis, and expected substantial sums to tolerate his existence among them; he would find himself taxed and hampered at every stage of his communications, and involved in litigation which ended only in his despair. Addis was always full of more or less undeserving Europeans who had been reduced to destitution by this process. There were a few mills, a brewery, a few plantations, whose white owners continued to struggle for a living; in the north an eminently workable potash concession was reduced to bankruptcy. In other parts of Africa Europeans had found things too easy; here conditions were deliberately made intolerable. The result was that the national resources of the country were unexplored and unexploited even to the extent that the Abyssinians imported tropical products, such as sugar, rather than adventure themselves into the lowlands where they might be produced or allow more enterprising races to undertake the work for them. Inevitably, the unknown became the focus for legends; frustrated cupidity acted as a spur to imagination, people spoke of vast deposits of gold and platinum, of untapped wells of oil, while the only foreigners, mostly Asiatic and Levantine, to make a living from the country were the traders and small monopolists, and they were in constant embarrassment through the difficulties put in their way by the courts of collecting their debts. Everyone who had any dealings with the Imperial Family— the Indian who took command photographs of the princesses, the Russian who put the electric lighting into the new palace, the dentist, the chef—were kept waiting hopelessly, indefinitely for their money. The rases and officials copied the Emperor. The law courts were conducted with the same policy. Decisions given in favour of foreigners were only after the maximum of delay, if at all, put into execution. Under the capitulations, generally known as the Klobukowski Treaty, special tribunals had been set up to deal with cases between Ethiopians and foreigners in which the respective consuls sat. It was the custom to balance the accounts periodically and pay to whichever party had the larger credit the balance in his country's favour. Shortly after the coronation, under the present régime, the time came to settle the score between the British consul at Addis Ababa and the Ethiopian officials; a large undisputed sum was outstanding in the British favour. The Ethiopian officials maintained that it was irregular for them merely to pay the difference; each side must appear with his full reckoning. Accordingly the British consul arrived with members of the Legation guard bearing in sacks of silver dollars the total sum due. It was counted out in the presence of the Ethiopians—a lengthy process—who then remarked that they had not their money with them; they would take the British dollars and bring theirs next week. The consul refused and the sacks were carried back to the Legation compound. A week later the Ethiopian judges said that they now had their money ready. The same procedure took place; the Ethiopians again tried to take the money, promising theirs on the next day; again the sacks were carried back under guard. At the third meeting the British consul said that he proposed to pay by cheque; the Ethiopians agreed, snatched the paper from his hands across the table and, with profuse promises that their money was on the way, watched him leave the court, satisfied that they had succeeded in outwitting the foreigner. The consul stopped the cheque by telephone, and from then onwards for two years the special tribunal ceased to sit.

Mildly comic incidents of this kind were of frequent occurrence in the very centre of Haile Selassie's government; prolonged and multiplied all over the country they assumed a more offensive complexion. The Soudanese and Kenya frontiers were kept in a state of expensive vigilance by their turbulent neighbours. But the British were a race whom, on the whole, the Abyssinians liked and respected; the Italians were suspected and despised; they were, moreover, a race whom recent developments of patriotic ardour, combined with the memory of past humiliations, made particularly sensitive to insult. They were a race whose colonial aspirations were concentrated in that part of the globe. Great Britain and France with their diffuse interests were not easily to be provoked to an unremunerative war. The Italians were waiting for an opportunity to demonstrate their new virility. The repeated grave annoyances were doubly offensive to them since, by the Treaty of Friendship of 1928, they had every reason to regard themselves as especially privileged.

It was evident, within six years of its having been made, that the Abyssinians had no intention of maintaining the spirit of that treaty. Italy had expected tangible commercial advantages. Her ambitions were clear and, judged by the international morality of America, Japan or any of the League Powers, legitimate. Abyssinia could not claim recognition on equal terms by the civilised nations and at the same time maintain her barbarous isolation; she must put her natural resources at the disposal of the world; since she was obviously unable to develop them herself, it must be done for her, to their mutual benefit, by a more advanced Power. By the 1928 Treaty, Italy believed that she had been chosen for this office. Abyssinia required technical advisers for her administration, whom Italy expected to supply; Abyssinia needed additional and cheaper means of access to the sea, which Italy offered through her colonies, granting a free zone in the port of Assab. In all these matters Italian expectations were disappointed. Little scope was given for Italian commercial enterprise. Of the many foreigners engaged by Haile Selassie as advisers and experts only one Italian was chosen and that for a minor post. The new arterial road, which was specifically provided in the 1928 agreement, joining Dessye with Assab was abandoned and, instead, Haile Selassie concentrated in opening communications with the British territories in Kenya and Somaliland. The construction of a wireless station at Addis Ababa was undertaken by an Italian company, heavily subsidised by the Italian government, but on completion was handed over to the management of a Swede and a Frenchman. A large hospital—the only building of any architectural merit in Addis Ababa—was erected with Italian money, partly voted by the government, partly subscribed by private Italian philanthropists, but pressure was exerted to prevent Abyssinians availing themselves of it. Italian social service throughout the country was suppressed; Ethiopians were forbidden to attend the consulate doctors; even Ethiopian cattle were kept from the Italian vets who were attempting to treat with prophylaxis the cattle plague that was ravaging the herds of both empires. The Ethiopian government persisted, as it had done for nearly forty years, in evading its promise to demarcate the Italian frontiers. Complaints of illegal imprisonment, injury and murder of Italian subjects accumulated and were left unsatisfied; insults to Italian diplomats and consuls and attacks on their property and servants went unpunished.

Some responsibility for the subsequent disaster must rest with the other European Legations at Addis Ababa, who constantly refused to take common action but pursued the old policy of competing for Ethiopian favour in their own small schemes of advantage. It is doubtful whether any warning was given to the Emperor of the change of temper between democratic and Fascist Italy; of the claustrophobia, aggravated by the universal economic depression, which now inclined her to welcome rather than shun an appeal to force. Whatever was said was qualified by the assurance that the Emperor was covered by the protection of the League and by the ignorant confidence of his army in their ability to defeat the Italians as they had defeated them before. It was in these circumstances, in December 1934, when Italy had finally despaired of achieving her objects by peaceful means and had already begun to sound the Powers tentatively about their attitude to her expansion in Africa; when she was actually in search of a diversion from internal distress, that the Abyssinians chose to attack the military post at Walwal.

It is uncertain how far this piece of folly was directed from Addis Ababa, and how far it was the spontaneous act of the troops on the spot. The committee which examined the evidence at Geneva came to no conclusion. What is certain is that it was not a tribal raid of the kind that was common along that frontier but a serious battle fought by a properly constituted Abyssinian force from the north.

Walwal is a watering-place and pasture without regular inhabitants, frequented at various seasons by the tribes of British and Italian Somaliland and the Ethiopian Ogaden. The treaties defining the frontier were mutually contradictory and the ground had never been surveyed, but the place undoubtedly lay in the Ethiopian sphere. Nothing, however, had been done by the Abyssinian authorities to make their possession in any way effective. By its character it was a natural battleground for tribal warfare, involving peoples under Italian protection, and in the absence of any Abyssinian police post the Italians had established one there, without protest of any kind, five years before. No attempt was made to conceal its existence, and the Anglo-Abyssinian boundary commission [1] who visited it on November 23 must

[1] I have never seen any satisfactory explanation of what this commission was doing there, 80 miles off its course.

have known what they would find. They arrived at the head of a large force—far in excess of any normal protective escort—which had assembled behind their caravan. Its numbers have been variously estimated; probably there were about six hundred Abyssinian soldiers, drawn from the garrisons of the Galla-Somali borders. Realising that there was going to be trouble, the British commissioners withdrew with their normal escort, leaving this extraordinary force behind to fight it out; there was thus no impartial witness to determine the disputed point of who fired the first shot. Whatever the Italian legal position, they were certainly on the defensive tactically. The battle took place on December 5 and the Abyssinians were defeated. It was then that they decided to resort to arbitration and the Italians decided to resort to war. There were attempts at ambush on Italian patrols in the Ogaden on December 28 and January 8, and on January 29 an attack in force on the Italian garrison at Afdub; both sides began to prepare for war on a larger scale; but while the Abyssinians enlisted European sympathy by a scrupulous regard for the formalities of peaceful negotiation, the Italians boasted from the first that they proposed to fight—in their own time and in the manner which suited them best.

No one except Signor Mussolini knows exactly what form he intended the war to take. There are indications that it was originally planned as a punitive demonstration; the transport and disembarkation of immense loads of war material was accomplished with great ostentation, but until the autumn of 1935, when hostilities had actually begun, little was done to improve the roads between Massawa and the front line. My own belief—and this is purely personal and conjectural—is that as late as the beginning of summer, 1935, Signor Mussolini had no intention of making war upon a national scale or of attempting the military conquest of the whole Ethiopian Empire. I believe that Italian agents throughout Ethiopia had been sounding the loyalty of the local chiefs, had paid large subsidies to them and had secured a system of treaties and verbal understandings which led them to expect a practically bloodless settlement. It was Signor Mussolini's hope that before Christmas his envoy at Geneva would be able to present the League with evidence of a series of voluntary submissions, and to claim that there had been no act of aggression or conquest—merely an exchange of allegiance by the people themselves; that all that was necessary to precipitate mass desertions was a demonstration of overwhelming force which would be performed mainly in the air. A few sharp encounters with modern methods of war would bring the Abyssinians to realise their necessarily inferior and dependent station; they were then to be left as a sovereign state, consisting of Shoa, Amhara, Gojjam and the greater part of Tigre. Adowa should remain in Italian hands as a monument that the defeat of 1896 had been avenged; the Abyssinian subject-races would be transferred to Italian protectorate. In Addis Ababa the Italian representative should assume a position similar to that once held by the British High Commissioner in Egypt; the internal order of the country should be taken from the charge of the local magnates and put under a national gendarmerie, officered by Italians; England and France should be allowed to enjoy the same position as they had occupied before except that Signor Mussolini was willing to facilitate the construction of the dam at Lake Tsana which had up till then been delayed by the Abyssinians. The neighbouring territories would have been saved much expense and anxiety through the establishment of an orderly rule on their frontiers; the subject peoples would have gained by changing to progressive and comparatively humane masters; the Abyssinians themselves would have preserved the traditional forms of their independence and participated in the profits resulting from the development of their resources.

This policy certainly underestimated the duplicity of the Abyssinian rulers with whom Italy had been in contact, and the confidence in their superiority of the Abyssinian troops, but I believe that the misfortunes that have fallen upon both peoples—the slaughter and terror on one side, the crippling expenditure on the other—are primarily due to the policy pursued by the British government.

The Emperor believed that if he could win the support of the League, there would be decisive action on his behalf; he transmitted this to his simpler subjects in the assertion that England and France were coming to fight against Italy, so that even those who had least love of Abyssinian rule feared to declare themselves against what seemed to be the stronger side.

The Italians, in the face of sanctions and a campaign of peevish and impotent remonstrance in England, felt their national honour to be challenged and their entire national resources committed to what, in its inception, was a minor colonial operation of the kind constantly performed in the recent past by every great Power in the world.

At the time of writing [1] the papers are filled with reports of the death agonies of the Abyssinian people and scholars are demonstrating in the correspondence column their ingenuity in composing Greek epitaphs for them. No one can doubt that an immense amount of avoidable suffering has been caused, and that the ultimate consequences may be of world-wide effect.

[1] April 1936.

II

ADDIS ABABA DURING THE LAST DAYS OF THE
ETHIOPIAN EMPIRE

I

IN the summer of 1935 the *Evening Standard* published a cartoon representing the Throne of Justice occupied by three apes who squatted in the traditional attitude, each with his hands covering his eyes, ears or mouth; beneath was the legend, " *See no Abyssinia; hear no Abyssinia; speak no Abyssinia.*"

This may have expressed the atmosphere of Geneva; it was wildly unlike London. There the editorial and managerial chairs of newspaper and publishing offices seemed to be peopled exclusively by a race of anthropoids who saw, heard and spoke no other subject. Few of them, it is true, could find that country on the map or had the faintest conception of its character; those who had read Nesbitt believed that it lay below sea-level, in stupefying heat, a waterless plain of rock and salt, sparsely inhabited by naked, homicidal lunatics; those who had glanced through Budge pictured an African Thibet, a land where ancient, inviolable palaces jutted on to glaciers,

an immemorial régime hedged by intricate ceremonial, a mountain solitude broken only by monastic
bells calling across the snowfields from shrine to
shrine; the editor of one great English paper believed—and for all I know still believes—that the
inhabitants spoke classical Greek.

But Abyssinia was News. Everyone with any
claims to African experience was cashing in. Travel
books whose first editions had long since been
remaindered were being reissued in startling wrap-
pers. Literary agents were busy peddling the second
serial rights of long-forgotten articles. The journal
of a woman traveller in Upper Egypt was advertised
as giving information on the Abyssinian problem.
Files were being searched for photographs of any
inhospitable-looking people—Patagonian Indians,
Borneo head-hunters, Australian aborigines—which
could be reproduced to illustrate Abyssinian culture.
Two English newspapers chose their special correspondents on the grounds that they had been born in
South Africa. In the circumstances anyone who had
actually spent a few weeks in Abyssinia itself, and had
read the dozen or so books which constituted the
entire English bibliography of the subject, might
claim to be an expert, and in this unfamiliar but
not uncongenial disguise I secured employment
with the only London newspaper which seemed to
be taking a realistic view of the situation, as a ' war
correspondent.'

There followed ten inebriating days of preparation,

lived in an attitude of subdued heroism before friends, of knowledgeable discrimination at the tropical out-fitters. There was a heat wave at the time (''Nothing to what *you're* going to, Sir,'' they said). I trod miasmic pavements between cartographers and con-sulates. In the hall of my club a growing pile of packing cases, branded for Djibouti, began to con-stitute a serious inconvenience to the other members. There are few pleasures more complete, or to me more rare, that that of shopping extravagantly at someone else's expense. I thought I had treated myself with reasonable generosity until I saw the luggage of my professional competitors—their rifles and telescopes and ant-proof trunks, medicine chests, gas-masks, pack saddles, and vast wardrobes of costume suitable for every conceivable social or climatic emergency. Then I had an inkling of what later became abundantly clear to all, that I did not know the first thing about being a war correspondent.

2

After the bustle, ten tranquil days on the familiar route. The *Golden Arrow* half seen through the feverish twilight of 6 A.M. Gerard Street gin; acquaintances on the boat (`` We are going Cannes. Where are you ? '' ''Addis Ababa ''); sleep between Calais and Paris; an acquaintance in the dining-car (``I am going to Antibes. Where are you ? '' '' Addis Ababa ''); cool early morning at the

Marseilles docks, succeeded by a day of burning heat; sailing at sunset. Five days in the Mediterranean, of calm water and cool breezes; the familiar depressing spectacle of French colonial domesticity on the Messageries decks; stud poker at night with two matey Americans, an exquisitely polite Siamese and a bumptious Dutchman. Port Said at midnight; Simon Arzt's coming to life; a fellow journalist slipping away to cross-examine the harbour master. Sultry days in the Canal; the Dutchman's manners at the card table becoming increasingly offensive. Finally, on August 19, Djibouti; the familiar stifling boulevards; spindly, raffish Somalis; the low-spirited young man at the Vice-consulate; the tireless, hopeless street pedlars; the familiar rotund Frenchmen, their great arcs of waistline accentuated with cummerbunds; the seedy café clientèle, swollen at this moment by refugees—Dodeccanean mostly—from up the line and by despondent middle-aged adventurers negotiating for Ethiopian visas; the familiar after-dinner drive to the café in the palm grove; the fuss about train and luggage. A torrid, almost sleepless night. On the 20th, shortly before midday, we crossed the Ethiopian frontier.

The occupants of the railway carriage were typical of the rising tide of foreigners which was then flowing from all parts of the world to the threatened capital.

There were six of us, sipping iced Vichy water from our thermos flasks and gazing out bleakly upon a landscape of unrelieved desolation.

One of them had been my companion from London, a reporter from a Radical newspaper. I saw him constantly throughout the succeeding months and found his zeal and industry a standing reproach. I did not know it was possible for a human being to identify himself so precisely with the interests of his employers. He never stopped working; he was continually jotting things down in a little notebook; all events for him had only one significance and standard of measurement—whether or no they constituted a 'story.' He did not make friends; he 'established contacts.' Even his private opinions were those of his paper; the situation, obscure to most of us, was crystal clear to him—the Emperor was an oppressed anti-fascist. His editor had told him that he must wear silk pyjamas under his clothes if he wished to avoid typhus; he never neglected to do so. He carried with him everywhere an iodine pencil with which he painted flea bites and scratches, so that he soon presented a somewhat macabre piebald spectacle. In the final reckoning he probably sent back sounder information than many of us.

My other colleague was a vastly different character. From time to time he gave us visiting cards, but we never remembered his name, and for the next few weeks he became a prominent and richly comic figure in Addis life, known to everyone as 'the Spaniard.' He was vivacious and swarthy and stout, immensely talkative and far from intelligible in English, French and German. His equipment, as he proudly admitted, was largely acquired at a sixpenny store. He changed his clothes in the train, putting on breeches and a pair of chocolate-coloured riding boots which laced up the front, and a Boy Scout's belt and revolver holster. He then placed a tin aneroid on the seat beside him and proclaimed the changes of altitude with boyish excitement, peeling and devouring one by one throughout the journey an enormous basket of slightly rotten bananas.

It was clear to us that Spanish journalism was run on quite different lines from English. From the moment we left Marseilles he had been composing articles for his paper—one about Haifa, two about de Lesseps, one about Disraeli. "I have a very good history of Africa in German," he explained. "When I have nothing to report I translate passages from that. Mine is the most important paper in Spain, but it is a great thing for them to send a correspondent as far as this. They must have news all the time." He had no cabling facilities at the Radio and was obliged to pay for all his dispatches in cash, a transaction which involved him in endless counting and recounting of coins and notes. While the rest of us were leading a life agreeably unembarrassed by the financial cares that occupy so much attention in normal travel, the Spaniard was in a chronic high fever of anxiety about his expenditure; for many days after his arrival at Addis Ababa he was to be found with a stub of pencil and sheet of paper working out how many thalers he should have got for his francs at Djibouti and brooding sceptically over the results; he was apparently an easy prey for the dishonest; his cabin, he complained, was rifled on board ship and a wad of money stolen; at Djibouti he had a still odder misfortune; he gave me his pocket-book to guard while he went for a swim and on his return maintained that a thousand francs had disappeared from it. He bewailed the loss at length and in piteous terms, saying that he was saving it for a present to his little daughter. But I made no offer to reimburse him and he soon recovered his jollity. It was a great surprise to him to discover that three of the English journalists beside myself were new and probably temporary members of our staffs and that all except one were entirely new to the work of foreign correspondent. " I am the most important and expensive man on my paper," he said.

" English editors would not send anyone whose life they valued on a job of this kind," we told him.

" I have my revolver. And the boots are snake-proof. How much do you think they cost ? "

Someone suggested ten shillings.

"*Very* much less," he said proudly.

He was one of the few people who, I really believe, thought that the coloured races were dark skinned because they did not wash. " Look at his black thumb holding my plate ! " he would exclaim with loathing when native servants waited on him. But he was of a volatile nature and his displeasure never lasted. He did not intend to stay long in Ethiopia, because, he explained, he was his paper's Paris correspondent and it was impossible to do both jobs satisfactorily at the same time. "I shall merely make a rapid tour of the front on a motor bicycle," he said.

In the absence of any more probable alternative, it was later put about in Addis Ababa, where everyone was credited with some sinister activity, that the Spaniard was a papal spy.

The fourth member of the party was a sturdy American doctor who had come to offer his services to the Ethiopian Red Cross. With him was Mr. Prospero, whom he had rescued from an indefinite sojourn in the Djibouti hotel. Mr. Prospero was photographer for an American news reel. A few weeks before he had been a contented resident in Japan, where he owned a house, a dog; had lately paid the last instalment on a saloon car, and employed his time making pictures of cherry blossom and court ceremonial. At a few hours' notice he had been whisked away from this life of lotus eating and deposited, penniless—his funds having been cabled in advance to Addis—at Djibouti, than which there can be no town in the world less sympathetic to strangers desirous of borrowing a railway fare. His life thereafter was a protracted martyrdom gallantly but gloomily endured, which seemed to typify the discouragement which in less degrees we all suffered. At Addis he was accommodated at the Imperial Hotel in a ground-floor room immediately next to the only

entrance; as more camera men arrived, they joined
him there with camp beds and mountains of technical
apparatus until the little room, heaped with cameras
and crumpled underclothes, packing-cases of film and
half-empty tins of baked beans, presented a scene
hideously compounded of workshop, warehouse and
slum dormitory. I saw Mr. Prospero constantly, and
always in distress; now soaked to the skin pathetically grinding the handle of his camera in an im-
penetrable pall of rain; now prostrate under the
bare feet of a stampeding mob, like a football in a
rugger scrum, now lamed, now groaning with
indigestion, now shuddering in high fever. He
became a figure from classic tragedy, inexorably
hunted by hostile fates. After we had been in
Addis Ababa some time a copy of a poster arrived
from America advertising his news reel. It represented a young man of military appearance and more
than military intrepidity standing calmly behind his
camera while bombs burst overhead and naked
warriors rolled interlocked about his knees. In
vast letters across this scene of carnage was printed :

" O.K., BOYS, YOU CAN START THE WAR NOW
PROSPERO IS THERE."

The sixth and by far the gayest of us was an
Englishman who was soon, suddenly, to become
world famous: Mr. F. W. Rickett. He had joined
our ship at Port Said and throughout the succeeding
week had proved a light-hearted companion. From

the first he was invested with a certain mystery. Anyone travelling to Addis Ababa at that moment attracted some speculation. Mr. Rickett spoke openly of a ' mission,' and when tackled by the Radical on the subject hinted vaguely that he was bringing Coptic funds to the Abuna. He spoke more freely about a pack of hounds which he had in the Midlands, and when, as often happened, he received lengthy cables in code, he would pocket them nonchalantly, remarking, " From my huntsman. He says the prospects for cubbin' are excellent." The Radical and I put him down as an arms salesman of whom large numbers were said to be frequenting Addis Ababa. In the gaudy reports of his concession which flooded the papers of the world a fortnight later great emphasis was laid upon Mr. Rickett's ' unobtrusive entrance ' into the country and his residence at ' an obscure boarding-house.' Nothing could have been further from his intentions or expectations. He had ordered the one luxury carriage of the Ethiopian railway and treasured the most extravagant hopes about its character—even to the belief that it contained a kitchen and cook. He had, in fact, very kindly offered me a place in it. But when we got to the station we found that we had to take our places in the ordinary coach. In the same way he had ordered a suite at the Imperial Hotel. It was only when we found there was no other accommodation, that we went to Mrs. Heft's excellent *pension*. Moreover, as will later appear,

he had no desire, once it was signed, to keep his
coup a secret. It was by chance that it became
the single sensational scoop of the entire war.
Mr. Rickett was far too genial to concern himself
with matters of that kind.

The day wore on, more oppressive after luncheon
at a wayside buffet; the little train jerked and
twisted through an unendurable country of stone
and anthills. There were no signs of rain here, the
sand was bare, the few tufts of scrub colourless as
the surrounding stone; the watercourses were dry.
At sunset we stopped for the night at Dire-Dawa, an
orderly little town created by and subsisting on the
railway; it was entirely French in character and
population, divided by the dry river bed from a
ramshackle native quarter. I remembered how
gratefully I had left it five years before. Now in the
cool of the evening, with the lights of the hotel terrace
revealing sombre masses of flowering bougainvillea it
seemed agreeable enough. The head of the railway
police came up from the station with us for a drink.
He was one of the new school of Ethiopian official—
clean shaven, khaki-clad, French speaking. He told
us the latest news from Europe. Mr. Eden had
walked out of the Paris discussions. That meant
that England was going to fight against Italy, he
said. "That depends on the League of Nations,"
we said.

"No, no. It is because you do not want Italy to

be strong. It is good. You know that Ethiopia cannot threaten you. We are friends. Together we will defeat the Italians."

We did not disabuse him; instead we accepted our temporary popularity as easily as we could, clinked glasses and drank to peace.

Next morning at dawn we resumed our places in the train and reached Addis that evening.

I little suspected what a large part in our lives that stretch of line was going to play in the coming months. I covered it six times before Christmas and learned every feature—the transition from desert to downland, the view of the lakes, the cinder fields, the Awash gorge, the candle-lit hotel at Awash where on every journey but this one the train deposited us for the night, the stations where there was an ostrich, a beggar who recited prayers, a little girl who mimed, the painted arch of the lake hotel at Bishoftou which told that the climb was nearly over and that we were in measurable distance of Addis, the silly coon-face of the ticket collector outside the window as he climbed along the running boards to enquire who wanted to lunch at the buffet. But at this time we all assumed that, when war was declared, we should at once be isolated. On the first day Awash bridge would be bombed and the line cut in a hundred places. The Abyssinians were at work already in the manner, at once both laborious and haphazard, which characterised all their enterprises, getting together materials for alternative bridges and loop lines, but no one had any reliance on them. We had all planned routes of escape to Kenya or the Soudan. At the beginning of October every train that left for Djibouti was reported as the last until even the most persevering among the journalists lost interest. If anything had been needed to rob the situation in which we found ourselves of any remaining vestige of heroic glamour it was this regular, unimpaired service to the coast. No one, except the few informed French officials, expected this. Of the various fates which from time to time we predicted for Haile Selassie—rescue by British aeroplanes, death in battle, murder, suicide—no one, I think, ever seriously suggested what was actually to happen; that in the final catastrophe, desperate and disillusioned, betrayed by the League, deserted by his army, hunted by insurgent tribesmen, with his enemies a day's march from the Palace and their aircraft regularly reconnoitring over his head, he would quietly proceed to the station, board the train and trip down to Djibouti by rail. The least romantic of us never suggested that.

3

Addis Ababa on the eve of war seemed little changed in character and appearance from the city I had known five years before. The triumphal arches that had been erected for the coronation had grown shabbier but they were still standing. The ambitious

buildings in the European style with which Haile
Selassie had intended to embellish his capital were
still in the same rudimentary stage of construction;
tufted now with vegetation like ruins in a drawing
by Piranesi, they stood at every corner, reminders
of an abortive modernism, a happy subject for the
press photographers who hoped later to present
them as the ravages of Italian bombardment. The
usual succession of public holidays paralysed the life
of the country; we arrived on the eve of one of them
and for two days were unable to cash cheques or
collect our luggage from the customs. There was
a new Palace and some new shops. The lepers,
driven into the villages for the coronation, had
returned; that was the most noticeable change.

The newspapermen in their more picturesque
moods used often to write about the cavalcades of
fighting men who swept through ' the narrow streets
of the mountain capital,' evoking for their readers
the compact cities of North Africa. In fact the
streets were very broad and very long. Everything
lay at a great distance from everything else. The
town was scattered over the hillside like the litter
of a bank holiday picnic party.

One chief thoroughfare, curving sharply where
it crossed the river, led from the old Gibbi (Menelik's
Palace) to the irregular space before the post office
which constituted the hub of the town. Here, on
a drab little balustraded concrete island, stood one
of the four public monuments of the town, a gilt

three-pointed star on a concrete pedestal. Two
rival cinemas stood on either side soliciting patronage
through the voices of two vastly amplified gramo-
phones, which played simultaneously from sunset
until long after midnight, when the hyenas and wild
dogs usurped the silence, howling over the refuse
heaps, disinterring the corpses in the public cemetery.
Other streets branched off from here, leading
variously to Giorgis (the Cathedral), the commercial quarter, the hotels and the wireless station.
A broad road led down to the railway, a strip of
tarmac down the centre, at the sides mule tracks
deep in mud during the rains, rutted and dusty
during the dry season. In front of the station stood
another monument, a gilt Lion of Judah. The third
was near Giorgis, an equestrian statue of Menelik,
which I had seen unveiled at the time of the coronation (it was a morning rendered remarkable by the
rivalry of two brass bands; at the moment of un-
veiling, as happens from time to time in more
northerly countries, the flag failed to respond and
had to be torn off in sections by a Greek contractor
on a step ladder; one fragment proved inaccessible,
a square of vivid green artificial silk which continued
to flutter gaily about the eyes and ears of the gilt
horse). The fourth was a concrete phallus copied
from one of the antiquities of Axum and, incongruously, embellished with a clock at the summit.
It stood in the cross roads at the furthest end of the
main thoroughfare, dominating a taxi rank of decrepit

and flea-infested vehicles which had now been relegated to the use of Asiatics. The taxis in the fashionable quarter of the town were also flea-infested, but brand new and as fast as the roads would allow. There was a great number of them, brought up by train, native driven, their fares so wildly augmented for the new arrivals that the old residents were obliged with the utmost reluctance to pursue their business on foot.

The frontage of the main streets was broken by many empty building lots and—a more depressing spectacle—by abandoned foundations and the ruins of recent fires. (An insurance company had lately begun operations in Addis Ababa and the result had been a holocaust of important business premises.) Between them stood shops, offices, cafés and private houses, for the most part of one storey, all roofed with corrugated iron, built of concrete or timber. A few shops had windows of plate glass. The most prosperous sold tins of food and bottles of deleterious spirits. A stationer's shop displayed European papers and indecent postcards; there were Goanese tailors and Armenian bootmakers; an iron-monger's dealing in frail-looking firearms and very solid knuckle-dusters; a German confectioner's; beyond the bazaar quarter stood the huge emporium of the firm of Mohamedally.

The entire trade of the town was in alien hands, for the most part Levantine and Indian. I do not think there was a single shop or office managed by

an Abyssinian. The artisans were Arab and Sikh.
Even the porters on the railway were Arabs. There
was no Abyssinian middle class. The lowest manual
labour and the highest administrative posts were
reserved for them; bullying and being bullied. They
had no crafts. It was extraordinary to find a people
with an ancient and continuous habit of life who had
produced so little. They built nothing; they made
no gardens; they could not dance. For centuries
Africa has offered Europe successive waves of æsthetic
stimulus. Of the gracious, intricate art of Morocco
or the splendour of Benin, the Abyssinians knew
nothing; nor of the dark, instinctive art of the
negro—the ju-ju sculpture, the carved masks of the
medicine man, the Ngomas, the traditional terrifying
ballet which the dancing troops carry from the Great
Lakes to the islands of Zanzibar and Pemba. To
lounge at the door of his hut counting his cartridges,
to indulge in an occasional change of wife, to have
a slaveboy in attendance to trot behind his mule
carrying his cheap Belgian rifle, to be entertained,
now and then, by his chief to a surfeit of raw beef
and red pepper and damp grey bread, to boast in his
cups of his own bravery and the inferiority of all
other races, white, black, yellow and brown—
these after centuries of self-development were the
characteristic pleasures of the Abyssinian.

In the Church alone his æsthetic feelings found
expression. Compared with the manifestations of
historic Christianity in any other part of the world,

West or East, the decoration was shoddy, the ceremony slipshod, the scholarship meagre, but, at least,
it was something unique in the life of the people.
By its interminable liturgy, its school of fine pen-
manship and direct didactic painting, its lore of
customary right and wrong, it fostered a tradition
independent of, and antagonistic to, the ideals of
Addis Ababa—the push and polish of the *Jeunesse
d'Ethiopie*.

Those who are inclined to lament the passing of
a low but individual culture should remember that
it was already marked down for destruction. In
Persia and Turkey, to-day, we see the triumph of
native progressive parties, accompanied by the swift
obliteration of native piety and of almost all that
made native life characteristic and beautiful. The
Abyssinian progressive party was still uncertain of its
strength. It aimed at breaking the influence of the
clergy; most of its members were personally
irreligious, but they had not yet begun openly to
attack the beliefs on which the influence of the
clergy was based. Specifically Christian formulæ
were still preserved in many of their utterances.
But the Church and the particular brand of development at which the *Jeunesse d'Ethiopie* aimed could
not have subsisted together. The people had been
tenacious of their faith against centuries of invasion;
they were bound to it by the routine and special
occasions of their life. It is probable that the
Jeunesse d'Ethiopie would have fallen. If they had

65

failed, Europe would have intervened. If they had succeeded, they would have created a country that was independent, powerful, uniform and utterly drab.

4

There were several hotels in Addis Ababa, all, at the time of our arrival, outrageously prosperous. The 'Splendide,' at which we all assumed we should stay—the Radical had had the name painted in large white letters on his medicine chest—was completely full with journalists and photographers living in hideous proximity, two or three to a room even in the outbuildings. It was a massive, shabby building of sepulchral gloom, presided over by a sturdy, middle-aged, misanthropic Greek, who had taken it over as a failing concern just before the troubles. There was something admirable about the undisguised and unaffected distaste with which he regarded his guests and his ruthless disregard of their comfort and dignity. Some attempted to be patronising to him, some dictatorial, some ingratiating; all were treated with uniform contempt. He was well aware that for a very few months nothing that he did or left undone could affect his roaring prosperity; after that anything might happen. The less his guests ate the greater his profits, and from his untidy little desk in the corner he watched with sardonic amusement the crowds of dyspeptic journalists—many of them elderly men, of note in their own country—furtively carrying into his dining-room paper bags of fresh bread, tins of tuck and pocketsful of oranges and bananas, like little boys trooping in to tea at their private schools. Mr. Kakophilos never apologised and very rarely complained. Nothing of the smallest value was endangered in the scenes of violence which became increasingly frequent as the journalists made themselves at home. When his guests threw their bedroom furniture out of the window, he noted it in the weekly bill. If they fired their revolvers at the night watchman he merely advised the man to take careful cover. Menageries of unclean pets were introduced into the bedrooms; Mr. Kakophilos waited unconcerned until even their owners could bear their presence no longer. His was the chief hotel of the town and nothing could shake its status. Here, intermittently, the government posted its *communiqués*; here the Foreign Press Association held its acrimonious meetings; here every evening, when the wireless station was shut, we all assembled, in seedy wicker chairs in the large, bare, flea-ridden hall, to drink and grumble.

The Deutsches Haus, where Mr. Rickett and I were taken, was humbler and very much more hospitable. It stood near the Splendide in a side street, but its immediate surroundings were not imposing. Opposite was a tannery run by a Russian Prince, from which, when the wind was in the wrong quarter, there came smells so appalling that we were obliged to shut our windows and scatter in different parts of the town;

67

sometimes a lorry of reeking pelts would be left all day at our gates; once, for some purpose connected with his hideous trade, His Highness acquired a load of decomposing cows' feet. He was a debonair figure, given to exotic tastes in dress. When he first arrived at Addis he was asked to luncheon at the British Legation and the guard turned out for him. A few days later he opened a house of ill fame. Now he was mainly, but not exclusively, interested in the fur trade. He often spoke wistfully of a convoy of girls who had been on order from Cairo since the battle of Walwal but were held up somewhere, mysteriously and unjustly, in the customs.

On either side of the Deutsches Haus stood the quarters of native prostitutes, single-roomed, door-less cabins from which issued occasional bursts of raucous squabbling and of more raucous light music. Cotton curtains hung over the entrances which were drawn back when the inhabitants were disengaged, to reveal a windowless interior, a wood fire, a bed and usually a few naked children and goats. In the old days the curtains bore the time-honoured device of the red cross, but lately a government order had caused it to be removed. It was still to be seen in the provinces, but at Addis only the upright remained and a cleaner strip where the bar had been unpicked. The ugliness of these women was a constant source of wonder to us, not, indeed, on account of their natural disadvantages, because that is a matter of common observation in their profession all over the world, but of their neglect of any possible means of embellishment. I asked my interpreter what were the charges at these houses.

" For me," he said, " it is a thaler because I am a British subject. If an Abyssinian gives a thaler he goes again and again until there is a quarrel."

Quarrels seemed fairly frequent, to judge by the sounds which greeted us at all hours of the day on the way to the Deutsches Haus.

But though the surroundings were forbidding, the hospitality inside the gates (which were kept by a grizzled warrior armed with a seven-foot spear) was delightful. Mrs. Heft was one of the Germans who had drifted to Abyssinia from Tanganyika when it was confiscated by the British government after the war. There were a large number of her compatriots in the town, mostly in very poor circumstances, employed as mechanics or in petty trade. The Deutsches Haus was their rendezvous where they played cards and occasionally dined. The Hefts could never quite get used to the disregard of small economies or the modest appetites of her new boarders. Many of our demands seemed to her painfully complex. " The journalists pay well," she confided. " But they are very difficult. Some want coffee in the morning and some want tea, and they expect it always to be hot." But she worked untiringly in our service.

She was a housewife of formidable efficiency. Daily from dawn until noon a miniature market was held on the steps of the dining-room. Half a dozen native hawkers squatted patiently, displaying meat, eggs and vegetables. Every half-hour she or Mr. Heft would emerge, disparage the goods, ask the price, and, in simulated rage, tell the salesmen to be off. Eventually, when it was time to start cooking luncheon, she made her purchases.

Mr. Heft had a deafening little car, which at any moment of the day or night he would take out for our use. There was also a hotel taxi, which the bearded chauffeur used as a crèche for his baby. When his services were required he would whisk the infant out of the back seat and nurse it as he drove.

There were two geese loose in the yard who attacked all comers. Mr. Heft was always promising to kill them, but they were still alive when I left the country. There was also a pig, which he did kill, from which Mrs. Heft made a magnificent abundance of sausages and patés. The food, for Addis, was excellent. Mr. Heft hovered over the tables at meal times watching all we ate. " No like ? " he would say, in genuine distress, if anyone refused a course. " Make you eggies, yes ? "

The Hefts' bedroom opened from the dining-room, and it was there that everything of value in the house was kept. If one wanted change for a hundred thaler note, an aspirin, a clean towel, a slice of sausage, a bottle of Chianti, the wireless bulletin, a spare part for a car, a pack of cards, one's washing or one's weekly bill, Mrs. Heft dived under her bed and produced it.

I always suspected that in his rare moments of leisure Mr. Heft was doing a little journalism on his own account. There were few people in Addis who, in course of time, did not find themselves on the pay roll of one or more of the various news agencies.

The Deutsches Haus soon became the headquarters of most of the English journalists and photographers. We employed our own servants, decorated our rooms with monkey-skin rugs from the Russian Prince and native paintings from the itinerant artists, and were, on the whole, tolerably comfortable. *The Times* and the Reuter's correspondents rented houses. The Americans, more Baedeker-minded, stayed resolutely with Mr. Kakophilos.

There were two places of entertainment in the town, *Le Select* and the *Perroquet*, usually known by the names of their proprietors, Moriatis and Idot. Both had a bar and a talking cinema. Mme. Idot had also a kitchen and put it about that her cooking was good. From time to time she would placard the town with news of some special delicacy— *Grand Souper*. *Tripes à la mode de Caen*—and nostalgic journalists would assemble in large numbers, to be bitterly disillusioned. She came from Marseilles, Mme. Moriatis from Bordeaux. They were bitter rivals, but while Mme. Moriatis affected ignorance of the other's existence, Mme. Idot indulged in free

71

criticism. "Poor woman!" she would say. "What does she think she is doing here? She should go back to Bordeaux. She has a face like Lent." M. Moriatis was a very handsome cad-Greek; M. Idot a hideous cad-Frenchman. Both, by repute, whipped their wives, but Mme. Idot professed to enjoy it. Mme. Idot shed an atmosphere of false gaiety, Mme. Moriatis of very genuine gloom. One talked gravely to Mme. Moriatis about the beauties of France and the wickedness of Abyssinian character; she was always apologising for the inadequacy of her entertainment and one tried to encourage her. "It is not *chic*," she would say very truly. "It is not as I should like it. If the Italians were here we should have dancing at the aperitif time and upstairs an hotel with bathrooms—completely European." Everyone pinched Mme. Idot and slapped her behind, told her that her films were unendurable and her wines poisonous. *Le Select* had pretensions to respectability and occasionally held charity matinées attended by members of the diplomatic corps. There was no nonsense of that kind about the *Perroquet*. Both prospered on the contrast, because, after an hour in either place, one longed for the other.

There were three hospitals in the town—two of them American, one Italian. There was a mosque and countless churches—Abyssinian, Armenian, Greek Orthodox, Catholic, Church of England, Adventist. There were government offices and the

ramshackle palaces of wealthy Abyssinian rases.
There was an hotel near the railway station, built
over a hot spring, where, if one could face the leper
who guarded its approach—a woman of nightmare,
unique even in a land of appalling spectacles—one
could get a bath. And behind and around all these
buildings lay the *tukals* of the native inhabitants,
clusters of thatched huts packed in the hollows and
gulleys which broke the hillside, among the great
groves of eucalyptus. They seemed to have little
part in the life of the city; one could live there
for weeks and scarcely be aware of their existence.
From them, in early morning, the crowds emerged
which all day long sauntered about the streets,
picking their way bare-footed from stone to stone of
the rough pavements. There was curfew an hour or
so after sunset; then any native was liable to arrest.
By dinner time they had entirely disappeared, like
office workers from the City of London, and the
streets were given up to aliens and hyenas.

5

Most visitors to Addis Ababa arrive feeling ill.
The sudden rise from coast level to eight thousand
feet, the change of temperature from the heat of the
Red Sea to the cold nights and sunless days of the
plateau in the rainy season, the food and, if they are
imprudent, the water they have consumed at the
railway buffets during the ascent, all contribute to
disturb the hardiest constitution. On this occasion

our distress was aggravated by the feverish and futile bustle in which all our colleagues appeared to be living, and the unplumbed lethargy of the native customs officials which prevented us getting to our luggage and warm clothes until late on the third day after our arrival. I had mild dysentery and a heavy cold, and lay in my room for two days, dizzy, torpid and acutely miserable, until a series of peremptory cables from Fleet Street roused me to a sense of my responsibilities: *Require comprehensive cable good colourful stuff also all news*, shortly followed by *Please indicate when can expect comprehensive cable*, followed by *Presume you are making arrangements getting stuff away* and *What alternative means communication in event breakdown?*

The method by which telegrams were distributed gave limitless opportunity for loss and delay. They were handed out to the messengers in bundles of about a dozen. The men were unable to read and their system of delivery was to walk round the town to the various hotels and places where foreigners might be expected to congregate and present their pile of envelopes to the first white man they saw, who would look through them, open any that might seem of interest, and hand back those that were not for him. Often it took more than a day for a message to reach us and, as the commands of Fleet Street became more and more fantastically inappropriate to the situation and the inquiries more and more frivolous, we most of us became grateful for a respite, which sometimes obviated the need of reply.

However, on the third day one of these messengers found his way to my room with the first, very reasonable request, so I left my bed and set out rather shakily into the pouring rain to look for ' colour.'

First steps as a war correspondent were humdrum —a round of the Legations with calling cards, a sitting at the photographers' to obtain the pictures needed for a journalist's pass, registration at the Press Bureau.

This last was a little tin shed at the further extremity of the main road. It might well have been classed among the places of entertainment in the town. Here morning and afternoon for the first six weeks, until everyone, even its organisers, despaired of it ever performing any helpful function, might be found a dozen or so exasperated journalists of both sexes and almost all nationalities, waiting for interviews. It was an office especially constituted for the occasion. At the head of it was a suave, beady-eyed little Tigrean named Dr. Lorenzo Taesas. He was a man of great tact and many accomplishments, but since he was also Judge of Special Court, head of secret police, and personal adviser to the Emperor, it was very rarely that he attended in person. His place was taken by another Tigrean, named David, equally charming, a better linguist, an ardent patriot, who was unable on his own authority to make the

most trivial decision or give the simplest information.
" I must ask Dr. Lorenzo," was his invariable answer
to every demand. In this way a perfect system of
postponement and prevarication was established. If
one approached any government department direct,
one was referred to the Press Bureau. At the Press
Bureau one was asked to put one's inquiry in
writing, when it would be conveyed to the invisible
Dr. Lorenzo. At this early stage the Abyssinians
had no reason to be hostile to the Press. Most of
them in fact—and particularly the Emperor—were
eager to placate it. But this was the manner in
which Europeans had always been treated in the
country. Just as many white men see a negro as
someone to whom orders must be shouted, so the
Abyssinians saw us as a people to be suspected,
delayed, frustrated in our most innocent intentions,
lied to, whenever truth was avoidable, and set against
one another by hints of preferential treatment.
There was no ill-will. The attitude was instinctive
to them; they could not alter it, and closer
acquaintance with us gave them good reason to
stiffen rather than relax.

Almost all those impatient figures on Dr. Lorenzo's
doorstep were after one thing. We wanted to get
up country. Travelling in Ethiopia, even in its rare
periods of tranquillity, was a matter of the utmost
difficulty. Many writers have left accounts of the
intricate system of tolls and hospitality by which the
traveller was passed on from one chief to another

and of the indifference with which the Emperor's *laissez-passer* was treated within a few miles of the capital. Now, with torrential rains all over the highlands flooding the streams and washing away the mule tracks, with troops secretly assembling and migrating towards the frontiers, with the subject peoples, relieved of their garrisons, turning rebel and highwaymen, the possibilities of movement in any direction were extremely slight. But, at any rate for the first weeks after our arrival, we most of us cherished a hope, and the Press Bureau constantly fostered it, that we should get to the fighting. No one ever got there. My last sight of Lorenzo, more than three months later at Dessye, was of a little figure, clad in khaki then in place of his dapper morning coat, surrounded by a group of importunate journalists in the Adventist Mission compound, promising that very soon, in a few days perhaps, permission would be granted to go north. Actually it was only when the front came to them, and the retreat of the government headquarters could not keep pace with the Italian advance, that any of them saw a shot fired.

But meanwhile there still lingered in our minds the picture we had presented of ourselves to our womenfolk at home, of stricken fields and ourselves crouching in shell holes, typing gallantly amid bursting shrapnel; of runners charging through clouds of gas, bearing our despatches on cleft sticks. We applied, formally, for permission to travel, absolving the government of all responsibility for our safety, and awaited an immediate reply.

The Radical, who knew his job, had no illusions of the kind. The court, the government offices and the Legations were the ' news centres.' His place was near the wireless office. Not so my immediate neighbour in the Deutsches Haus, an American who proclaimed his imminent departure for the Tigre. A squad of carpenters was noisily at work under our windows boxing his provisions, his caravan of the sturdiest mules was stabled nearby. He had already discarded the dress of a capital city and strode the water-logged streets as though he were, even at that moment, pushing his way through unmapped jungle. Poor chap, he was one of the group surrounding Lorenzo at Dessye.

6

It was the general belief, shared by the Abyssinians, that the main campaign would be fought in the south. There would be a small advance in great strength from Asmara, a ceremonial entry into Adowa, the erection of some kind of monument to the fallen in the war of 1896; then troops would be transferred by sea to Mogadishu and from there would drive up the comparatively easy country of the Fafan valley to Jijiga, Harar and the railway. This was what the military experts predicted. In the circumstances, with the northern roads impassable, the best plan seemed to be to move south and see as much as was

possible of the line of this advance. Three journalists had already been some way, one of them a
considerable way, in that direction. Facilities were
becoming rarer and we were warned by David that
we should now get no further than Harar; but I had
hopes, based on my acquaintance with the officials
of five years back, that the men on the spot might
prove more amenable. Even if we were obliged to
stay in Harar there seemed a prospect of better news
than in Addis, for there were exciting rumours from
there of Italian propaganda among the Mohammedans.
In Addis everything seemed to be at a standstill.

Mr. Rickett, it is true, held out hopes of a story.
He was clearly up to something and drove off every
now and then to interview such very dissimilar
dignitaries as the Abuna [1] and Mr. Colson, the
American financial adviser of the Emperor. I thought
it impertinent to inquire further. On the second
day of our visit he had promised me an important
piece of news on Saturday evening. Saturday came
and he admitted, rather ruefully, that he had not
been able to arrange anything; it would probably
be next Wednesday, he said. It seemed clear that
he was involved in the endless postponements of
Abyssinian official life, from which the American
doctor was also suffering with undisguised annoyance,
and that in ten days' time I should find him at the

[1] The Egyptian head of the Abyssinian Church. His predecessor
had been a man of great personal influence, but the present Abuna
was unambitious and far from well.

Deutsches Haus, still negotiating. Accordingly, with Patrick Balfour, an old friend who had preceded me as correspondent for the *Evening Standard*, I decided to leave by the Monday train.

In the meantime we attempted to collect what little news there was in Addis. Troops were drilling on many of the roads; there was no other place for them, for the fields were water-logged and there was no dry parade ground. A great deal was written about the smartness of the Imperial Guard—the Belgian-trained force of Haile Selassie's own creation, which had been in existence for about six years. They shaved their faces and wore tidy uniforms; the cavalry rode well-matched, well-groomed ponies, the infantry usually marched in step and refrained from chatter when standing at attention. They formed an outstanding contrast to the general shabbiness of the town and to the wild feudal levies. But they would have gained little credit as a contingent at an O.T.C. camp in England, and in comparison with the Somali Camel Corps or the K.A.R. they were rabble.

There were volunteers also from the town and surrounding district about three thousand strong, who were paid a thaler or two a week, when they had not forfeited the sum in fines for lateness or undiscipline. There was something pathetically futile about their training. They lived at home with their wives and, at dawn, began to pour in, many from farms at some distance. When they had been paraded and counted they were marched two miles to the old armoury and issued with rifles. These had to be returned again at evening and carefully counted. There was an inherent disposition for the Abyssinian, as soon as he was given a new rifle, to take to the hills with it. The least that might be expected was that he would shoot up a *tedj* house. So a large part of the day was occupied in distributing and collecting the arms. The remainder was spent in arms drill and march discipline on the European model. As there was practically no road outside the city where four men could march abreast, and as the one quality in which Abyssinian troops were sensationally effective was in their habit of movement—breaking up over miles of country, foraging and resting at will, now strolling pensively, now trotting, covering prodigious distances daily—this forming of fours, dressing by the right, keeping step, wheeling and halting to command seemed quite without purpose.

And yet it is hard to suggest what could have taken its place. There was far too little ammunition for target practice. The country all round was a swamp where it was impossible to exercise in open order. They had only a few weeks to prepare. They were mostly detribalised by their residence in and near the capital; the drill at least taught them to obey their new superiors. It also acted as an intoxicant and spur to patriotism. The children took it up, and could be seen drilling one another in front of their homes. Even some of the women, in the houses round the Deutsches Haus, might be seen saluting and practising right and left turns. But it seemed an incomplete preparation for meeting a modern mechanical army.

There was a meeting of high-born ladies in premises that had formerly been a night club to discuss the formation of a local Red Cross unit. Patriotic speeches were made and a subscription collected. There were rumours brought me by a sibilant Greek most of which were so obviously false as to need no investigation. There was a morning of great excitement when it was believed, wrongly, that a member of the Italian Legation had been ambushed by natives. There were strongly supported and quite untrue reports that a legion of Egyptian volunteers was on its way to fight for the Abyssinians. There were untrue stories of a munition factory that was being opened by an English engineer, and of an army of women that was secretly drilling in the provinces. There was a genuine financial crisis and a run on the bank. There were demands from Fleet Street for daily items of ' spot news.'

It was with great relief that, on Monday morning, August 26—in the entirely purposeless secrecy with which the journalists in Addis invested all their movements—Patrick and I set out for Harar.

III

HARAR AND JIJIGA

I

THE train to Diredawa was full of refugees. All the
trains at this time carried a fair number. There was
never, except immediately after the outbreak of the
war, any real panic, but the men of the foreign
community were being quietly advised by their
consuls to get their families out of the country, and
those who could were winding-up their affairs and
following. Only the Italians had been told to go
quickly, and most of them had gone before I came.
They left in high spirits, confident of a speedy and
glorious return. The Greeks from Rhodes and the
Dodeccanese formed a more sombre body. Many of
these had been born in Abyssinia; almost all had
come to the country as Greek or Turkish nationals.
It was the only home they had known; they were
artisans earning a better living than they could have
got among their own people. Then, by changes in
the map that were incomprehensible to them, they
found that they had suddenly become Italians, and
now they were being hustled down to the coast with

the prospect of being recruited into labour gangs or soldiers to fight against the country of their adoption. There were several of them in our train, wistfully sucking oranges in the second-class coach.

In the first class were a large party of Levantine women and children, plump and pallid as though modelled in lard. After a noisy and emotional leave-taking they subsided into their places and sobbed quietly for an hour, then began to cheer up and expand, opened their cases and produced thermos flasks and bags of sweetmeats until they gradually spread over the whole coach an atmosphere of sticky domesticity.

The only male was one of the former mystery men of Addis, who was reputed to be an Englishman, an engineer, and the future organiser of the Emperor's munition factory. He told us that he found journalists very inquisitive people, but his story, for what it was worth, had now ' broken,' so that we were able to join him at cut-throat bridge without embarrassing him with further questions. After fifteen hours we reached Diredawa and Mr. Bololakos' hotel. Early next morning the mystery man and the emigrants proceeded to the coast and Patrick and I were left to make our arrangements for going to Harar.

Until three years before, the journey took two days. One rode out on mule-back, first for a sultry hour along the river bed, then by a precipitous track up the hillside among thorn and boulders, out into open downland, through corn crops and coffee fields to the rest house on Lake Harramaya, where one spent the night; on next day, along the broad, frequented caravan route to the walled city. Now there was a motor road.

It was this road which constituted one of the particular grievances of the Italians. In the 1928 agreement the Abyssinians had promised to make their second outlet to the sea from Dessye to Assab; instead they had chosen to link the railway with Berbera in British Somaliland. A stream of motor lorries now followed this route, carrying out coffee and skins, bringing in, it was believed, arms and ammunition. It formed, too, the main line of communication with the Ethiopian Ogaden, the channel by which supplies would reach troops at Sasa Baneh and Gerlogubi. Jijiga was the junction where the ways divided, one to Hargeisa and British Somaliland, the other down the Fafan valley; it was therefore expected to be the main objective of the autumn campaign.

For centuries before Menelik Harar was an independent Emirate, a city state founded by Arabs from across the Red Sea, who held sway over a large and fertile province inhabited by peaceable Moslem Gallas. They held the caravan route between the coast and the interior and made their city the emporium of a rich trade in coffee and slaves. The Harari people spoke their own language, wore a distinctive costume, and exhibited a very high standard of culture in comparison with their rough neighbours. They were rigid in their faith and hostile to foreign influence. The Emir's family claimed high, Sheriffian descent and already showed signs of decadence when Burton—the first white man in their history—visited them in the middle of the last century. He came, as he admits in his account of the expedition,[1] with the intention of preparing the way for English occupation. His description of the city and its people was no doubt somewhat modified by his desire to make out a good case for interference. He represents them as vicious, tyrannical and rather squalid. The Hararis, naturally enough, look back to the days of their independence as a golden age, the Bagdad of Haroun al Raschid. No doubt it differed little from the other Moslem Sultanates which once covered the African coast and trade routes; a despotism that was sometimes benevolent and sometimes oppressive according to the disposition of the reigning monarch, but qualified always by the integrity of Khoranic law; Harar had its shrine which formed a centre of pilgrimage; its market where goods of exotic value were displayed; a place of riches and security which easily became a splendid legend among the surrounding barbarians. Even in 1935, after a generation of Abyssinian misrule and Indian and Levantine immigration, it retained something of the gracious fragrance of Fez or Meknes.

Burton's ambition was disappointed. During the brief experiment of Khedivial imperialism, Harar

---

[1] *First Steps in East Africa*, by Sir Richard Burton.

fell under Egyptian rule; for a few months it was garrisoned by Indian troops and flew the Union Jack. Then it was abandoned to its fate and captured by the Shoans under Menelik.

In the first stages of the Franco-Ethiopian Railway it was proposed to join Harar with Djibouti, but the work stopped short at Diredawa, the enterprise came in danger of failure, and, when the line was continued, it was run direct to the capital. Harar was then under French influence; a French mission and leper settlement were established there and the town became the headquarters of romantic smugglers of whom Rimbaud is the most illustrious. But its wealth rapidly declined. The railway had usurped the place of the camel-track as the main trade route. The Shoan rulers fastened themselves upon the dying body and drained it of vitality. The Emir's family lived in poverty and obscurity; the position of the sheiks became purely titular. Abyssinians lounged and swaggered in every office; as the revenue from trade fell, the duties were increased to support them; the Galla peasants, bringing their baskets of produce to market, found their meagre profits absorbed in customs-dues. The Abyssinian garrison lived on the free labour of the conquered people; the Harari women carried their water and wood. Christian manners and morals [1] defiled the holy places.

---

[1] Khoranic law forbids prostitution. The rows of *tedj* houses in Harar were all staffed by Abyssinian women. Under Abyssinian rule the liquor trade became a valuable source of revenue. The older

When I visited the town in 1930 it was clearly declining fast. The fringe of houses immediately inside the walls were empty and ruinous, as though, like the lepers that thronged the streets, Harar were already dead and decaying at its extremities.

The motor road did something to revive its importance, but at the expense of its charm. We left Diredawa shortly before midday, having been delayed by the necessity of obtaining passes to cross the provincial boundary. Patrick and I and his servant had now been joined by another Englishman, an old acquaintance named Charles G., who had come out primarily in search of amusement. He had arrived in the small hours of the morning, the train from Djibouti having been twice delayed— once by a two-mile wash-out of the track, once by the impatience of the engine-driver, who had started off after the midday halt leaving all his passengers still lunching at the buffet. There was also a youthful and very timid Abyssinian nobleman, who wanted a lift and raised entirely vain hopes of his being useful to us.

We left in two cars and, twisting and groaning up the countless hairpin bends and narrow embankments of the new road, were very soon at the top of the pass, which formerly had taken four hours of

---

Hararis complained bitterly of the consequent demoralisation of the younger generation. It is worth noticing, however, that Burton, fresh from the austere standard of Arabia, was shocked by the almost universal drunkenness he found in Harar.

arduous riding. Here was a military post, a barricade and new corrugated-iron gates, which were later described by many poetic correspondents as '' the ancient ' Gates of Paradise.' ''

They certainly emphasised the contrast between the Harar province and the surrounding wilderness. Behind lay the colourless, empty country which one saw from the train; mile after mile of rock and dust, anthill and scrub, and, on the far horizon, the torrid plain of the Danakil desert, where the Awash river petered out in a haze of heat. In front, beyond the surly Abyssinian guard, the uplands were patterned with standing crops, terraces of coffee, neat little farms in flowering stockades of euphorbia, the pinnacles of their thatched roofs decorated with bright glass bottles and enamelled chamber-pots. We passed one considerable village, dominated, as all such places were, by an Abyssinian squatter, and in less than four hours after our departure from Diredawa were in sight of the walls and minarets of Harar.

Perhaps I had been unduly eloquent in describing to my companions the beauties that awaited us. I had come to Harar, as Patrick and I were coming now, fresh from the straggling, nondescript, tin and tarmac squalor of Addis Ababa, and it had seemed like a city from the ' Arabian Nights.' Five years' absence had enhanced the glamour of that revelation. I spoke of it as a place of gardens and good manners and fine craftsmanship and described how, when the five great gates were closed at sunset, I had set out, heavily armed, with an Armenian publican, through a labyrinth of pitch-black streets, to a wedding party, where on a herb-strewn floor, in soft lamplight and clouds of incense, I had seen modest, light-hearted girls dancing formal and intricate figures. I had talked at some length about those girls; they had all the slender grace of the Somalis, their narrow hips, broad, straight shoulders and high, pointed breasts, but instead of their sooty, monkey faces had skins of warm golden-brown and soft, delicately carved features; they wore their hair in a multitude of plaits and covered it with brilliant silk shawls; another shawl was bound under their arms, leaving the shoulders and arms bare, and from knee to ankle were revealed slim calves, in tight trousers of bright spiral stripes, like sugar-sticks in a village post office. Their feet and the palms of their hands were dyed with henna. They were the débutantes of the town, unmarried girls of good family, the bridesmaids at the coming wedding. It was a unique spectacle for a Moslem city.

After all I had remembered, and all I had said, the reality was a little disappointing. There had been changes. The first sight to greet us, as we came into view, was a vast, hideous palace, still under construction; a white, bow-fronted, castelated European thing like a south coast hotel. It stood outside the walls, dominating the low, dun-coloured masonry behind it. The walls had been breached and, instead

of the circuitous approach of mediæval defence, the
narrow, windowless lane which had led from the main
gates, under the walls, bending and doubling until it
reached the centre of the town, a new, straight track
had been driven through. There was an hotel, too,
built in two stories, with a balcony, a shower-bath
and a chamber of ineffable horror, marked on the
door, *W.C.* It was kept by a vivacious and avaricious
Greek named Carassellos, who, everyone said, for no
reason at all, was really an Italian. This building,
where we took rooms, had been erected immediately
in front of the Law Courts, and the space between
was a babel of outraged litigants denouncing to
passers-by the venality of the judges, the barefaced
perjury of the witnesses, and the perversions of the
legal system, by which they had failed in their suits.
About twice every hour they would come to blows
and be dragged inside again by the soldiers to
summary punishment.

But the main change seemed to be in the pro-
portions of Abyssinians to Hararis. It was at the
moment, by all appearance, an Abyssinian town.
Great numbers of troops were being drafted there.
A Belgian training school was established. Abyssinian
officials had been multiplied for the crisis, and with
their women and children filled the town. The
Hararis were rapidly melting away; those that could
afford it, fled across the frontiers into French and
British territory, the majority to the hills. They
were a pacific people who did not want to get

involved on either side in the coming struggle; particularly, they did not want their women to get into the hands of the Abyssinian soldiers. In place of the lovely girls I had described, we found the bare, buttered, sponge-like heads, the dingy white robes, the stolid, sulky faces and silver crosses of the Abyssinian camp followers.

That afternoon the Abyssinian youth we had conveyed from Diredawa brought three educated friends to tea with us. It was a very dull little party. We learned later that here and in Addis Ababa any native who was seen conversing with a white man was liable to immediate arrest and cross-examination about what had been said. This restricted social intercourse to an exchange of the simplest commonplaces. Our guests wore European clothes, hats and shoes. I was unable to place one of them and asked him, as delicately as I could, whether he were Mohammedan or Christian. "I do not believe any of that nonsense," he said. "I am educated."

Later the chief of the police dropped in for some whiskey. He was an officer of the old school, greatly given to the bottle. He was suffering at the time from a severe cold and had stuffed his nostrils with leaves. It gave him a somewhat menacing aspect, but his intentions were genial. Very few journalists had, as yet, visited Harar, and the little yellow cards of identity from the Press Bureau, which were an object of scorn in Addis, were here accepted as being evidence, possibly, of importance.

Patrick's servant, whose French was fluent but rarely intelligible, acted as interpreter. That is to say, he carried on a lively and endless conversation, into which we would occasionally intrude.

" What is he saying, Gabri ? "

" He says he has a cold. He hopes you are well."

Then they would carry on their exchange of confidences. The end of this interview, however, was a promise that we should have a pass to take us as far as Jijiga.

2

Next day Fleet Street asserted itself again. A cable arrived for me saying, *Investigate Italian airplane shot down Harar*. There was absolutely no truth in the report. Had anything of the kind happened, the town would have been buzzing with the news. But the morning had to be spent disproving it. I visited the Italian consulate—furtively, because an incessant watch was kept at the gates—learned the latest uncompromising utterances from Rome which had just come over the wireless, and left by a side door in the compound.

There were more signs of military activity at Harar than in Addis. In the plain outside the walls two or three hundred camels were waiting to be moved south as transport animals, while in an outdoor circus ring Somalis were training others for riding. About five thousand Shoan troops were being drilled in Belgian methods and, in imitation of them, a company of Harari youths, fired with an uncharacteristic and very brief enthusiasm, had taken to marching about for an hour each morning, before they went to work. The Emperor had visited Harar a few weeks before, as he did yearly, for the province was a personal fief granted by Menelik to his father, and had attempted with some apparent success to conciliate Moslem opinion. There were promises of a new deal in the south and the creation of a Moslem Ras. Prayers were being offered in the mosques for Abyssinian victory and two sheiks sent round the tribes to preach a holy war against the Europeans. It was not until much later, on my return to the district, that I began to suspect how superficial this harmony was. At the moment everyone we met was anxious to impress on us the reality of Ethiopian unity. We were told of great numbers of deserters who were coming over from Italian Somaliland with their rifles and ammunition to offer their services to the Emperor. Actually, I think, in these weeks immediately before the outbreak of war there was a steady trickle across the frontier in both directions. The Somalis are a moody people who had little affection for either conqueror. They were ready to enlist temporarily with anyone who would give them a new rifle. The propaganda department of both sides, throughout the autumn and early winter, until Desta's defeat in January made it apparent which was the winning side,

were constantly issuing lists of the Somali chiefs who
had made their submission or organised a revolt in
the rival territories.

3

During our day of waiting for permission to go to
Jijiga, Patrick and I each engaged a spy. They were
both British ' protected persons,' who had for a
long time made themselves a nuisance at the Consulate. That was their only point in common.

Mine, Wazir Ali Beg, was an Afghan, an imposing
old rascal with the figure of a metropolitan policeman
and the manner of a butler. He wrote and spoke
nearly perfect English. At some stage of his life he
had been in British government service, though in
what precise capacity was never clear—probably as a
consulate dragoman somewhere. Lately he had set
up in Harar as a professional petition writer. He
put it about among the British Indians, Arabs and
Somalis who thronged the bazaar that he was a man
of personal influence in the Consular Court, and thus
induced them to part with their savings and brief
him to conduct their cases for them. To me he
represented himself as the head of a vast organisation
covering the Ogaden and Aussa countries. He never
asked for money for himself but to ' reimburse '
his ' agents.' On the occasion of our first meeting
he gave me an important piece of news: that a party
of Danakil tribesmen had arrived at Diredawa to
complain to the Governor of Italian movements in

their territory; a force of native and white troops
had penetrated the desert south-west of Assab and
were making a base near Mount Moussa Ali. It was
the verification of this report, a month later, which
provoked the order for general mobilisation and
precipitated the war. Wazir Ali Beg had a natural
flair for sensational journalism and was so encouraged
by my reception of this report that he continued to
recount to me by every mail more and more improbable happenings, until, noticing letters in his
scholarly hand addressed to nearly every journalist
in Addis Ababa, I took him off my pay roll. He then
used my letter of dismissal to put up his prices with
his other clients, as evidence of the sacrifices he was
making to give them exclusive service.

Patrick's spy was named Halifa, but he was soon
known to the European community as Mata Hari.
He was an Aden Arab whose dissolute appearance
suggested only a small part of the truth. He
approached us that evening without introduction
on the balcony of the hotel, squatted down on his
haunches very close to us, glanced furtively about
him, and with extraordinary winks and gestures of
his hands expressed the intention of coming with us
to Jijiga as interpreter.

His frequent appearances at the Consular Court
were invariably in the capacity of prisoner, charged
with drunkenness, violence and debts of quite
enormous amounts. He made no disguise of the
fact that most of his recent life had been spent in

gaol. When he found that this amused us, he giggled about it in a most forbidding way. He wore a huge, loose turban which was constantly coming uncoiled like the hair of a drunken old woman, a blue blazer, a white skirt and a number of daggers. Gabri, Patrick's Abyssinian servant, took an instant dislike to him. " Il est méchant, ce type arabe," he said, but Gabri, once outside the boundaries of his own country, was proving a peevish traveller. He did not at all like being among Mohammedans and foreigners. Harar he could just bear on account of the abundance of fellow countrymen, but the prospect of going to Jijiga filled him with disgust. The chief of police had already given us two effeminate little soldiers, who trotted at our heels wherever we went, weighted down by antiquated rifles, looking as though they would burst into tears at every moment of crisis. We felt we could do with an addition to our party, so Mata Hari was engaged. Our association with him did us no good in the eyes of the chief of police, and largely contributed, I think, to the subsequent expulsion of Charles G. ; but he added vastly to our amusement.

4

After protracted negotiations we had taken seats in a coffee lorry, bound for Hargeisa. There were the usual delays as the Somali driver made a last-minute tour of the town in the endeavour to collect additional passengers, and it was soon clear that we should not reach Jijiga by nightfall. Our two soldiers began nervously to complain of danger from brigands, but the journey was uneventful and we reached Jijiga, hungry and shaken, at ten o'clock that evening. For the first half the road ran through hill country, eminently suitable for a guerilla defence: the surface was abominable and almost every mile we passed through narrow defiles where a charge of dynamite could hold up a mechanised column; the hillside was strewn with boulders and densely overgrown with bush, affording limitless cover. It seemed the sort of country that a handful of men could hold against an army.

Later in the afternoon we emerged into the open plain. It seemed easy to predict the course of the war—the rapid occupation of Jijiga, a pitched battle beyond, ending in an overwhelming victory for the Italians, wild acclamation at Rome and the expectation of the fall of Harar; then a resolute rearguard action in the hills, indefinite delay, stubborn, expensive fighting while the long line of communication was constantly harassed by Ogaden tribesmen; then the rains again, and withdrawal to winter quarters in Jijiga. How wrong we were !

Rain came on at sunset and for four hours we made slow progress. The headlights pierced only a few feet of darkness; we skidded and splashed through pools of mud. Our driver wanted to stop and wait for dawn, saying that, even if we reached Jijiga, we should find ourselves locked out. We induced him to go on and at last came to the military post at the outskirts of the town. Here we found another lorry, full of refugees, which had passed us on the road earlier in the day. They had been refused admission and were now huddled together in complete darkness under sodden rugs, twenty or thirty of them, comatose and dejected. Our soldiers climbed down and parleyed; the driver exhibited the consular mailbag which he was carrying; Patrick and I produced our cards of identity. To everyone's surprise the barrier was pulled back and we drove on to the town. It was to all appearances dead asleep. We could just discern through the blackness that we were in a large square, converted at the moment to a single lake, ankle-deep. We hooted, and presently some Abyssinian soldiers collected round us, some of them drunk, one carrying a storm lantern. They directed us into a kind of pound; the gates were shut behind us and the soldiers prepared to return to bed.

There was no inn of any kind in Jijiga, but the firm of Mohamedally kept an upper room of their warehouse for the accommodation of the Harar consul on his periodic visits. We had permission to use this and had wired the local manager to expect us. His representative now appeared in pyjamas, carrying an umbrella in one hand and a lantern in the other. "Good night," he said, greeting us. "How are you?"

Fresh trouble started, which Mati Hari tried to inflame into a fight, because the soldiers in command refused to let us remove our bags. They had to be seen by the customs officer, who would not come on duty until next morning. As they contained our food, and we had had nothing to eat since midday, the prospect seemed discouraging. The Indian from Mohamedally's told us it was hopeless and that we had better come to our room. Mata Hari, Charles and I set out with one of our own soldiers to find the customs officer. We knocked up his house, where they refused to open the door but shouted through the keyhole that the customs office was at the French House. A handful of Abyssinians had now collected in the darkness. Mata Hari did all he could to provoke them to violence, but our Harari guard was more conciliatory and eventually we were led, through what appeared to be miles of mud, to another house, which showed a light and a posse of sentries. The nature of the ' French House ' was not at the moment clear. Sounds of many loud voices came from the interior. After Mata Hari had nearly got himself shot by one of the sentries, the door opened and a small Abyssinian emerged, clean shaven, dressed in European clothes, horn-spectacled; one of the younger generation. We later learned that he was new to his position, having spent the previous year in prison on a charge of peculation. He came with us to the lorry, apologising in fluent French for the inconvenience we had suffered. Our bags were surrendered and the Indian led us to our room, where, after supper, we slept on the floor until daybreak.

5

One of the wonders of travel is where native servants sleep. They arrive at any hour in a strange place and seem immediately to be surrounded by hospitable cousins-in-law, who embrace them, lead them home and for the rest of the stay batten upon one's stores. Our party broke up and disappeared cheerfully into the night; all except Gabri, who did not like Jijiga. He was intensely zenophobic where Somalis were concerned; he would not eat anything himself, saying that the food was not suitable for an Abyssinian; he nearly starved us by refusing to buy provisions on the grounds that the prices were excessive.

Mati Hari seemed to have slept in the mud, to judge by his appearance next morning, but perhaps he had merely found his fight. He came to our room in a kind of ecstasy, almost speechless with secrecy. He had news of the highest importance. He could not say it aloud, but must whisper it to each of us in turn. Count Drogafoi, the French Consul, had been thrown into prison. We asked him to repeat the name. He shook his head, winked and produced a stub of pencil and a piece of paper. Then, glancing over his shoulder to make sure he was not observed, he wrote the word, laboriously, in block capitals, DROGAFOI. It was to Drogafoi's house, he said, that we had been the night before. They were going to shoot Drogafoi that day. They had also arrested twelve Roman Catholics; these would be sewn up in skins and burned alive. There were four Maltese Popes in the town. They would probably be shot too. He would return shortly, he said, with further information, and with that and another meaning wink he tip-toed downstairs.

In a somewhat puzzled state of mind we sat down to a breakfast of tinned partridge and Chianti. While we were still discussing what, if any, possible truth could be concealed in this story, the customs officer, our friend of the night before, came to introduce himself by name—Kebreth Astatkie—and to inquire about our welfare. Dedjasmach Nasebu, the Governor of Harar, was in Jijiga that day, he told us, on his way south, and would be pleased to see us. Accordingly we set out on foot for the Gibbi.

Rain had stopped and the town presented a more cheerful appearance. It consisted of a single main square and two side streets. It had been laid out, not many years back, by the father of the young man we had brought from Diredawa. It served two purposes; a caravanserai on the Berbera-Harar road and military outpost and administrative centre on the fringe of the Ogaden. The Gibbi and Mohamedally's warehouse were the only buildings of more than one storey. The single European in the town, besides the mysterious Drogafoi and the Maltese Popes, was a Greek, whom Mata Hari pointed out to us, riding a bicycle.

"That is the Alcohol," he explained; an imposing title which, we found later, meant that he owned the local liquor monopoly.

We also discovered the identity of the Maltese Popes; they were four Franciscan friars who ran an impoverished little mission—a cluster of native huts, half a mile outside the town.

The Gibbi, like most Abyssinian official buildings, was a nondescript assembly of tin-roofed sheds, the largest of which had some upper rooms, reached by an outside staircase. Two half-grown lions were tethered outside the main door; the slave in charge wrestled with one of them for our benefit, and was rewarded with a thaler and a deep scratch on the thigh. There was the inevitable small army of ragged retainers, squatting on their heels, nursing their old rifles.

We were first shown into the presence of the governor of Jijiga, Fitaurari Shafarah, an officer of the old school, who sat, surrounded by local notables, in a very small room, hung with carpets; the shutters were closed and the atmosphere stupefying. He was a grizzled, gloomy little man who had been present at the battle of Walwal and had gained some discredit there, through being discovered, at the height of the action, squatting in his tent selling cartridges to his own troops. (It was not so much the trade itself that was resented as the fact that he put up the price when the Abyssinians seemed to be in difficulties.) His own interpreter introduced us, and after the exchange of a few civilities we sat in unbroken silence for rather more than half an hour. Eventually we were led into the open and upstairs to Nasbu's quarters. The Dedjasmach wore European uniform and spoke French. Like everyone else in Abyssinia who spoke French—with the single exception of the Emperor—he was clean shaven. He was well up in European affairs. We drank coffee together and discussed the constitution of the Committee of Five, the Committee of Thirteen, the Council of the League, and such topics as, in those days, seemed important.

Patrick then asked him what truth there was in the story that a Frenchman had been arrested in Jijiga.

"A Frenchman arrested?" he inquired with innocent incredulity. "I will ask about it."

He clapped his hands and sent a servant for Kebreth. They talked together for a few seconds in Amharic, discussing, presumably, what it was wise to give away; then he said, "Yes, it appears that something of the sort has occurred," and proceeded to tell us the whole story, while Kebreth produced from various pockets about his person a collection of all the relevant documents.

Drogafoi was a Count Maurice de Roquefeuil du Bousquet, who had come to Ethiopia nine years before in search of a livelihood; for the last three years he had been working a mica concession a few

miles out of Jijiga; three months ago he had married
a French widow from Diredawa. For some time
the police had been keeping a watch on his house.
He was said to live in guilty splendour, but when
Patrick and I visited his home later we found two
simple and clearly impoverished little rooms. The
main cause for suspicion was the fact that Somalis
from the neighbouring tribes resorted there, with
whom he could have had no legitimate business. On
the day before our arrival, an elderly Somali woman
had been arrested leaving his house and, when she
was searched, a film tube was found in her armpit,
which, she confessed, she was taking to the Italian
Consulate at Harar. Kebreth showed us the contents:
a snapshot of some motor lorries and five pages of
inaccurate information (of the kind which Wazir Ali
Beg used regularly to write to me) describing the
defences of Jijiga.

The Count and Countess had been arrested and
their house searched. Kebreth said it was full of
correspondence with Italian officers across the
frontier, and of the names of native agents who were
now being rounded up. He showed us the Count's
passport and finally the Count himself, who, with
his wife, was now under guard in an outbuilding of
the Gibbi. As a large proportion of the Count's
agents were boys who had been educated at the
mission school, unfounded suspicion had also fallen
upon the Franciscan friars. We took photographs
of the Gibbi and the Count's house, of the lion cubs

and the place of his imprisonment, of the slave in charge of the lions and the captain of the guard. Kebreth gave us a postcard of the Count posed against a studio background of drapery and foliage which he had confiscated among other more incriminating papers. A dramatic moment came when we expressed a wish to photograph the detective responsible for the arrest.

"You wish to photograph the detective?" said Kebreth. "He stands before you. It was I."

So we photographed Kebreth too, beaming through his horn-rimmed spectacles, and returned to Mohamedally's with the feeling that we were on to a good thing. It seemed to have all the ingredients of a newspaper story—even an imprisoned 'bride.' Moreover, there was no possibility of any other journalist having got it. We happily imagined cables arriving for our colleagues in Addis. '*Badly left Roquefeuil story*' and '*Investigate imprisoned countess Jijiga.*' It was now Friday morning. If we were to reach the Saturday papers it must be cabled by seven o'clock. Patrick and I feverishly typed out our reports while Charles engaged a car to take them to the nearest wireless station at Hargeisa, in British Somaliland, and Kebreth obligingly made out a pass for his journey.

6

When our cables were safely on their way, Patrick and I walked out into the town and there had another stroke of good luck. It was midday and the people

were trooping into the little mosque to their prayers.
A car drove up and there emerged a stocky figure in
a black cossack hat. It was Wehib Pasha, a Turkish
veteran of the Gallipoli campaign, one of the major
mystery men of the country. He had left Addis in
the greatest secrecy. There had been rumours that
he was bound for the Ogaden. Some said he was on
a religious mission, to preach a Moslem crusade
against the Italians; others that he was to be the
new Moslem Ras, whose appointment was hinted at.
Patrick had interviewed him in Addis and found him
profoundly uncommunicative.

His disgust at seeing us was highly gratifying. He
shot into the mosque and sent his secretary-companion
—an elegant Greek youth with a poetic black beard
and immense, sorrowful eyes—to inform us that we
were not to follow him about, and that if we took
any photographs he would have our cameras destroyed.
We sent Mata Hari into the mosque after him and
told him to make inquiries in the market about what
the Pasha was doing. The reply, which we got
some hours later, disentangled from Mata Hari's
more obvious inventions, was that the Pasha had
recruited a large labour gang and was leaving next
day for the south in a train of lorries, to dig lion
pits for the Italian tanks. This was the first news,
I think, which anyone got of the construction of
the famous defensive line which was believed to be
holding up Graziani's Northern advance for the
entire war. Actually these well-planned earth-
works were never used, for instead of an orderly

retreat, the Abyssinians fell back in hopeless rout and could not be persuaded to man them.

Feeling that our trip to Jijiga had been a triumphant success, Patrick and I made our arrangements with a half-caste lorry driver to return next day to Harar. There remained the delicate question of whether or no we should tip Kebreth. Gabri and Mata Hari, when consulted, said of course all officials must be tipped on all occasions; Gabri alone showed some anxiety that we would give too much. Accordingly when Kebreth came in that evening for a drink with us, Patrick produced a note and with great tact suggested that we should be glad if he would distribute a small sum to the poor of the town in acknowledgment of our enjoyable visit.

Kebreth had no respect for these euphemisms; he thanked us, but said with great composure that times had changed and Ethiopian officials now received their wages regularly.

Five hours' delay next morning in getting on the road. Our half-caste driver made one excuse and then another—he had to take some mail for the government, he was awaiting another passenger, the municipal officer had not yet signed his pass. At last Mata Hari explained the difficulty; there was shooting on the road; a handful of soldiers in the manner of the country had taken to the bush and were at war with the garrison. "This driver is a very fearful man," said Mata Hari.

Presently, when the half-caste had at last been

taunted into activity by our staff, the danger passed.
Less than a mile outside the town we met soldiers
coming back, dragging some very battered prisoners.
" Perhaps they will be whipped to death. Perhaps
they will only be hanged," said Mata Hari.

We lunched on the road at de Roquefeuil's mica
works—a dingy little jumble of sheds and a derelict
car. To our embarrassment the owner himself
suddenly appeared under the guard of two lorry
loads of soldiers. He had come to remove his
personal belongings before being sent north. He
sent out a message to us, to remind us that we were
on private property. We drove on and arrived at
Harar in the late evening.

We were still in a mood of self-approval. We
wondered whether any of our messages had yet
arrived in London and whether Patrick had got in
first with the Saturday evening edition, or I on
Monday morning. We expected cables of congratu-
lation. There was a cable for me. It said, '*What do
you know Anglo American oil concession?*' Evidently our
messages had been delayed; but as there was no possible
competitor, we were not alarmed. I replied, '*Apply
local agent for commercial intelligence Addis,*' and, still
in good humour, went up to dine at the Consulate.

Next morning there was another cable, a day old:
'*Must have fullest details oil concession.*' I replied:
'*Absolutely impossible obtain Addis news Harar.*' Before
luncheon there was a third: '*Badly left oil concession suggest your return Addis immediately.*'

It was now clear that something important had happened in our absence, which eclipsed our stories of Roquefeuil and Wehib Pasha. A two-day train left Diredawa for Addis on Tuesday morning. In low spirits Patrick and I arranged for our departure.

Harar had suddenly lost its charm. News of the events at Jijiga had filtered through in wildly exaggerated forms; the town was inflamed with spymania. Mata Hari was promptly gaoled on the evening of his return. We bought him out, but he seemed to expect hourly re-arrest and became completely incoherent with secrecy. The chief of police may have had some reprimand for allowing us to go to Jijiga or perhaps it was only that his cold was worse; whatever the reason, his manner had entirely changed towards us and he was now haughty and suspicious. Mr. Carassellos was in a condition of infectious agitation. Half his friends had just been arrested and cross-examined under suspicion of complicity with de Roquefeuil. He was expecting the soldiers to come for him any minute.

Roquefeuil and the native prisoners arrived on Sunday night. Throughout the day on Monday, Mata Hari popped in on us with fragments of unlikely news about his trial; that he was in the common prison, that the Emperor was coming in person to supervise his execution; that he had boasted, " In seven days' time this town will be in the hands of Italy and I shall be avenged." But the story had lost its interest for us.

7

No one in Harar knew anything about an oil
concession. The first information we received was
at Diredawa, where a young official explained that the
Emperor had leased most of the country to America.
At Awash we learned that Mr. Rickett was associated
with the business. At Addis, on Wednesday night,
we found that the story was already stale. Patrick
and I, the Reuters and *The Times* correspondents had
all been away. The *Morning Post* correspondent had
not yet arrived; thus the Radical and the *Daily
Telegraph* correspondent were the only English-born
journalists in Addis. They and the American
agency, Associated Press, had had the scoop to
themselves. It was a sensational story which, for
a few days, threatened to influence international
politics.

Mr. Rickett, as the agent of a group of American
financiers, had secured from the Emperor a concession for mineral rights of unprecedented dimensions.
The territory affected was that bordering on the
Italian possessions over which the Italian troops
would presumably seek to advance, and which,
presumably, they hoped to annex. The conces-
sionaires admitted absolute Abyssinian sovereignty
over the area and held it on a direct lease from
the Emperor. Much, perhaps most, of the rights
involved had already been ceded from time to time
to other interests, but it was in keeping with

Abyssinian tradition to disregard this. The significant feature, at the time, was the fact that Mr. Rickett was an Englishman, and that in the early reports his principals were described as an Anglo-American company. Apprehensions were immediately aroused in Italy, and to a less degree in France, that England, who was at the moment adopting an increasingly censorious attitude towards Italian ambitions, was herself bent on economic annexations in Ethiopia, and was merely using the League of Nations to gain commercial preference. In fact there was absolutely no truth in this, although it was, in the circumstances, a very natural suspicion. Mr. Rickett had not called at the Legation and the British Minister in Addis was completely unaware of his existence. During his stay he had, to my knowledge, met only one British official, and him the most junior, at dinner with Patrick and myself, when their conversation had been exclusively frivolous. No English capital, I believe, was involved in the venture. The purity of English motives was completely unaffected by the Rickett concession. There is, however, some room for reflection on the Emperor's behaviour.

It is popular now to regard him as completely ingenuous and completely dignified; a noble savage betrayed by his belief in the reality of the white man's honour. The Rickett concession shows him in a somewhat different form. It was made in direct contradiction to the previous policy of his reign, at the moment when he was declaring in highly felicitous and highly impressive terms an absolute and exclusive reliance on the Covenant of the League. He had already appealed to America as a signatory of the Kellogg Pact and learned that he could expect no support there. He was now attempting to buy that support. It was a shrewd attempt, but it came too late. Had the concession been made in 1934, it is difficult to see how the United States government could have permitted Italian occupation. As it was, in September 1935, with war already inevitable, the States Department at Washington intervened against him and forbade the ratification of the concession. By doing so they virtually recognised Italy's right to conquer, for, while he was still a sovereign ruler, they refused to recognise the Emperor's right to grant concessions within his own dominions. The Emperor had reverted to the traditional policy of balancing the self-aggrandisement of the white peoples one against another, and it failed. After that he was left with no cards to play except international justice, collective security and the overweening confidence of his fighting forces. He played the first two astutely enough; the third turned out to be valueless. No possible reproach can attach to him for his negotiation with Mr. Rickett. It might have proved masterly. But it does to some extent dispel the sentimental haze which, to liberal eyes, threatens to obscure his highly complex character.

IV

WAITING FOR THE WAR

ON our return to Addis Ababa we found the temporary white population still further increased. Of my original companions Mr. Rickett and the American doctor had both left; the one happy in the brief delusion that his mission had been a success, the other fully conscious of failure and indignant at the neglect and suspicion of the Abyssinian officials whom he had hoped to help. Their rooms at the Deutsches Haus were immediately snapped up. All the hotels were already overcrowded, the Splendide was a slum, the tide of journalists was still in flood. A week later (New Year's Day, 1928, in the Abyssinian calendar, which had fallen behind the rest of Christendom during the centuries of isolation) another boat train arrived, packed with pressmen, including two internationally celebrated correspondents of the Hearst organisation. Two more trains before the outbreak of war brought up the number of accredited journalists and photographers to rather more than a hundred. They showed almost every diversity which the human species produces.

There was a simian Soudanese, who travelled under a Brazilian passport and worked for an Egyptian paper; there was a monocled Latvian colonel, who was said at an earlier stage of his life to have worked as ring-master in a German circus; there was a German who travelled under the name of Haroun al Raschid, a title, he said, which had been conferred on him during the Dardanelles campaign by the late Sultan of Turkey; his head was completely hairless;. his wife shaved it for him, emphasising the frequent slips of her razor with tufts of cotton-wool. There was a venerable American, clothed always in dingy black, who seemed to have strayed from the pulpit of a religious conventicle; he wrote imaginative despatches of great length and flamboyancy. There was an Austrian, in Alpine costume, with crimped flaxen hair, the group leader, one would have thought, of some Central-European Youth Movement; a pair of rubicund young colonials, who came out on chance and were doing brisk business with number-less competing organisations; two indistinguishable Japanese, who beamed at the world through horn-rimmed spectacles and played interminable, highly dexterous games of ping-pong in Mme. Idot's bar. These formed an exotic background that was very welcome, for the majority of the regular pressmen were an anxious, restless, mutually suspicious crowd, all weighed down with the consciousness that they were not getting the news. They were expected to cable daily (all, that is to say, except the Spaniard, who, born in a happier and more leisured tradition, was content to post occasional thick packages of closely written manuscript), and the wireless station could only cope with the accumulations of copy by periodic closures.

The Americans were, on the whole, in easier circumstances, for their Press has created so voracious an appetite in its readers for impertinent personal details, that they can even swallow such information about the people who are employed to discover it. They were thus able to glut the service with expansive pages of autobiography about their state of health and habits of life, reactions and recreations, while the more practical Europeans were kept in pursuit of ' spot news.'

It was a disheartening quest. The situation throughout the whole of September was perfectly clear. Everyone was waiting for Italy at her own convenience to begin the war. There were committee meetings and conversations in Europe. News of them was published belatedly in our cyclostyle bulletin at the wireless office. No one, least of all the Abyssinians, believed they would deflect the Italians from their intentions. Until an ' act of aggression ' had actually taken place nothing could be done ; it would then appear what sort of support, if any, Great Britain and France were prepared to give. It was probable, as in fact occurred, that news of the beginning of hostilities would be published in Europe before we heard of it in Addis Ababa.

Meanwhile we were required to provide daily items of interest to keep public attention engaged.

There were reports from all over the country of extensive troop movements. The order for general mobilisation had not been made, but the local chiefs were collecting forces and moving them as un-ostentatiously as possible towards various points of concentration. A strong party, headed by Ras Moulungeta, were known to be in favour of imme-diate general mobilisation. The Emperor's policy at the moment was to avoid any movement that the Italians could interpret as being aggressive or menacing; it was believed that the order had been signed, printed, and then suspended. The news of its promulgation was cabled back almost daily by one or other of the special correspondents: '*War drums beating in the North—the Emperor raises the Standard of Solomon.*' Almost daily enquiries came from Fleet Street, '*What truth general mobilisa-tion?*' Like almost every important event in the war it was so often anticipated and so often denied that, when it actually happened, it had lost all its interest.

Occasionally troops came through Addis and entrained for Diredawa, but for the most part they remained out of sight. It was reported that in many places they had come without provisions and were plundering the farms on their route; in the Galla country, in particular, there had been serious disturbances and some loss of life. But there was no

possibility of leaving the city to investigate. No
answer was given to our applications for leave to
travel. We were obliged to rely for information
about what was happening in the interior upon the
army of Greek and Levantine spies who frequented
Mme. Moriatis's bar. Most of these men were
pluralists, being in the pay not only of several
competing journalists at once but also of the Italian
Legation, the Abyssinian secret police, or both.
They were equally ignorant, but less scrupulous
than ourselves. We could retail their lies, even
when we found them most palpable, with the quali-
fication, "It is stated in some quarters" or "I was
unofficially informed." There is a slight difference,
I discovered, in the professional code of European
and American journalists. While the latter will not
hesitate, in moments of emergency, to resort to
pure invention, the former must obtain their lies at
second hand. This is not so much due to lack of
imagination, I think, as lack of courage. As long as
someone, no matter how irresponsible or discredited,
has made a statement, it is legitimate news, but there
must always be some source, "which has hitherto
proved satisfactory," on which the blame can later
be laid.

The rains showed no signs of lifting, but they
provided another topic for our cables; grey clouds
hung low over the city, shutting out the surrounding
hills; at irregular, incalculable intervals they broke
in a deluge which rang so loud on the iron roofs as

to stop conversation during the day, and at night to give the illusion that one was travelling by train through a tunnel; there was little drainage in the town, and during the storms many of the side streets became cataracts; there was often thunder and sometimes hail; but now and then, once a week perhaps, there would be a few minutes' fitful sunshine and a patch of blue sky. That provided a story. Some correspondents described crowds of natives gathering, gazing up, apprehensive that a fleet of aeroplanes might emerge and begin the bombardment. (It is interesting to remember, in view of the outcry of pained surprise which later greeted the practically bloodless bombardment of Harar, that at this time almost everyone in Addis, Abyssinian and foreign alike, expected that the capital would immediately become a target not only for bombs but gas. Most of the population dug shelters in their gardens; others were made by the municipality; instructions were issued to the population that they were to take cover in the hills; many of the more timid correspondents shifted their quarters on the outbreak of war and slept with gas masks beside their beds.)

The railway station was a centre of minor information. An increased service was running at the time and trains left for the coast two or three times in the week. All had refugees on board—one day the women of the Swedish community, another the German—as the consulates arranged for the evacuation. Half the white population and practically all the Press were on the platform for each departure. There was seldom any very sensational occurrence; sometimes an Indian would be arrested smuggling dollars; there were always tears; once or twice an Abyssinian dignitary left on an official mission, attended by a great entourage, bowing, embracing his knees, and kissing him firmly on his bearded cheeks. At any time there was a fair amount of rough and tumble at the Addis terminus between Arab porters and station police. This served to give colour to the descriptions of panic and extravagant lamentation which were dutifully cabled to Fleet Street.

The arrivals in the evening were more interesting, for anyone visiting Addis at this season was a potential public character, perhaps another Rickett. Two humane English colonels excited feverish speculation for a few days until it was discovered that they were merely emissaries of a World League for the Abolition of Fascism. There was a negro from South Africa who claimed to be a Tigrean, and represented another World League for the abolition, I think, of the white races, and a Greek who claimed to be a Bourbon prince and represented some unspecified and unrealised ambitions of his own. There was an American who claimed to be a French Viscount and represented a league, founded in Monte Carlo, for the provision of an Ethiopian *Disperata* squadron, for the bombardment of Assab. There was a completely unambiguous British adventurer, who claimed to have been one of Al Capone's bodyguard and wanted a job; and an ex-officer of the R.A.F. who started to live in some style with a pair of horses, a bull terrier and a cavalry moustache—he wanted a job too. All these unusual characters were good for a paragraph.

The more respectable soldiers of fortune were, as was traditionally right, of Swiss nationality. Several of them secured posts of responsibility. There was also a gang of Belgian ex-officers, who were a great embarrassment to the charming Belgian minister, the *doyen* of the Addis diplomats. For five years there had been an official military mission from Belgium, seconded from their regiments to train the Imperial Guard. These were under orders to leave the country in case of war. The newcomers were there in defiance of their superiors. Some were Congo veterans, some young subalterns in search of adventure. They were engaged for vague general services and given quarters in the Empress's bathhouse, from which they emerged now and then in parties of half a dozen, to sit, a gloomy, uniform row in white bum-shavers, along Mme. Moriatis's bar. Their presence was not recognised by their fellow officers of the official mission; few of them were even given any serious occupation. In a few weeks their enthusiasm for the Abyssinian cause was noticeably cooler.

The government offices, particularly the Gibbi and the Foreign Office, were places which the

Radical described as 'News Centres.' It was frequently necessary to visit them to test the opinion of 'official circles' on the various proposals for a peaceful settlement which periodically cropped up as rumour in Europe and were urgently transmitted to us by wireless. These were disheartening expeditions. The official one sought was seldom available; one waited about in corridors and anterooms thronged with squatting, sodden, undisguisedly hostile soldiers, eventually to be received by some irresponsible, infinitely evasive deputy. The inaccessibility of the officials was due partly to their natural bent towards prevarication, but more to the lack of competent personnel, which was fatal to the Addis bureaucratic system. Half the officials were men of hereditary eminence and imperturbable, aristocratic lassitude; they spent the greater part of their day in eating and sleeping and when disturbed gave either of the traditional excuses that they were at prayer or had taken their *kosso*. The two or three comparatively businesslike men—the handful of genuine exponents of the ideals of the *Jeunesse d'Ethiopie*—were given such a multiplicity of posts that they had time for none of them. In this way urgent business was indefinitely held up, while parasites like ourselves were left in complete confusion.

There was also a mysterious and, I am now inclined to believe, non-existent force of Yemen Arabs which made a fitful appearance in our despatches. By some accounts they were still in the Yemen and were waiting orders for the attack from the Imam of Sana. They were to cross the Red Sea in a fleet of dhows, fall upon Assab and massacre the garrison, then join with the Aussa Sultan in a drive up the Italian coastline as far as Massawa. Another version had it that they were already in Addis, organised as a fighting corps. They were constantly reported as parading at the palace and offering their arms and fortune in the Emperor's service. There was in fact a number of venerable old traders from the Yemen, dotted about the bazaar quarter. If two of them sat down together for a cup of coffee it was described as a military consultation.

By every post, until I told him to stop, Wazir Ali Beg sent me a budget of news. Like our own reports, some of it was fantastic rumour, some trivial gossip, with, here and there embedded, a few facts of genuine personal observation.

' *An Arab sweet seller of Diredawa,*' he wrote, ' *left here for Djibouti about a month ago. Some Italian engaged him and gave him some packets of mortal poison and a big sum of money. This man was instructed to put each packet of poison in Water Reservoir of Diredawa. A Somali woman gave information about this to the Abyssinians. Many poison packets and a sum of 5200 francs were found on this Arab. He has been taken in chains to Addis Ababa. He is very short of stature and his hair have turned gray. The Emperor has rewarded this Somali woman and ordered that she be paid a sum of $1000.*'

When news was scanty he would sometimes fill up his page with such items as ' *News has been given me just now that the Somalis number 15 thousand men and there is no account of the number of Abyssinians going from all sides,*' or with darker hints: ' *I have news in my possession of the utmost importance. I have not forgotten your instructions, these news will be very dangerous to put on paper. I may only tell you these in person or send a special messenger.*'

On the last occasion he wrote to me—three weeks before the outbreak of hostilities—he reported a battle: ' *The Manager of Messrs. Mohamedaly and Co. and another trader informed me that there was news of a big clash between Somalis, Dankalis and white Italian soldiers near Assab. 500 white wounded soldiers were brought to Djibouti and 200 Italians are reported dead. If I had money I would at once have gone to Djibouti myself. But I trust these gentlemen as they are men of position.*' I had less trust than Wazir Ali Beg in these gentlemen of position, and as this letter was shortly followed by the suggestion of an enormous increase in his retaining fee and the assertion, which I knew to be false, that he had declined several offers of profitable employment from other journalists, I decided to drop him. He had no difficulty in finding other correspondents and, as the situation became darker and reporting more speculative, Wazir Ali Beg's news service formed an ever-increasing part of the morning reading of the French, English and American newspaper publics.

Whenever Mata Hari was out of prison, he too wrote. Patrick has already published the correspondence elsewhere, but, with his permission, I cannot forbear to quote a few extracts.

'THE ETHUPIAN NEWS OF THE 11TH SEPTEMBER

Troubles at 3 p.m.

Soldiers. *Fieghts near Bazara doors some of the Soldiers entered Bazara house as some brack heads bloods come out . . .*

Dagash Mazh *said the Ethupian troops will assault the Italian troops before the time of the rain . . .*

Dagash Mazh *regarding to the lecture of the 8th advise the soldiers, regret to say, at 3 p.m. the soldiers to their misfortune and endignity on the peoples, robing the vegetables, etc.*

Truck *passed on to leg of one Somalee.*

News *from the Arabic news papers, the warfare will be between six Governments shortly.*

Somali Merchant Mahmood Warofaih *made trench in his garden and put his money, few day repeat to see his money and not found, at once come mad.*'

This last trouble was by no means peculiar to Mahmood Warofaih. During the crisis it seemed to be happening all over the country. The gardener at the Deutsches Haus suffered in exactly that way and showed every sign of losing his reason until, to the disappointment of the other servants, who were enjoying the spectacle immoderately, Haroun al Raschid charitably reimbursed him.

The Foreign Press Association held occasional meetings, which until its final dissolution became increasingly disorderly as the weeks of proximity and competition produced an elaborate web of personal and racial antipathies. The meetings took place at the Splendide Hotel, in the evening when the wireless was shut, or was supposed to be shut, for the day. Discussion was bilingual and required constant interpretation. The intention was to establish a method of negotiation with the Ethiopian government. The result was to destroy whatever slight unity among themselves, or prestige among the officials, the journalists ever possessed. The meetings, however, were highly enjoyable, having a character of combined mock-trial and drinking bout. The Americans and French did most of the talking; the English endeavoured to collect the subscriptions and maintain some semblance of constitutional order. The Spaniard was elected a member of committee, with acclamation. The Radical made a conscientious and rather puzzled treasurer. The Americans were facetious or ponderously solemn, according as their drink affected them. There was one of them who was constantly on his feet crying: "Mr. Chairman, I protest that the whole question is being treated with undesirable levity." Every now and then the French walked out in a body and formed an independent organisation.

Our chief function was to protest. We 'protested unanimously and in the most emphatic manner' or we ' respectfully represented to the Imperial Government ' that the cabling rates were too high, that the Press Bureau was inconveniently situated and inadequately staffed, that a negro aviator had insulted a French reporter, that preferential treatment was given to certain individuals in the despatch of late messages, that the official bulletins were too meagre and too irregular; we petitioned to be allowed to go to the fronts, to be told definitely whether we should ever be allowed to go there. No one paid the smallest attention to us. After a time the protesting habit became automatic. The Association split up into small groups and pairs protesting to one another, cabling their protests to London and Geneva, scampering round to the palace and protesting to the private secretaries of the Emperor at every turn of events. But that was later; in these early days the Foreign Press Association showed some of the lightheartedness of a school debating society.

One of the events which attracted most attention was the arrival, early in September, of the reinforcements to the Sikh guard at the British Legation. As the constituents of this force had been exactly and publicly specified some time before in London, it was odd to see the ingenuity with which journalists sought to conceal themselves about the station and transcribe the names on the officers' uniform cases. One even hired a balcony overlooking the line and sat there all day in the hope of seeing their train come in.

It had been decided, with a minimum of common sense, that the arrival should be kept secret; the train, which was known to have left Diredawa, was left in a siding, some way down the line, until nightfall, when all the approaches to the station and Legation were elaborately cleared. If a simple statement, such as was made in London, had been issued, describing the numbers and equipment of the company, there would have been little excitement aroused. As it was, in a population like that of Addis, credulous, suspicious and given to the most extravagant exaggerations, wild rumours were circulated and believed. The Emperor had given repeated assurances, pledging his personal honour for the safety of all Europeans in his country. When eventually he fled precipitately, throwing open his arsenal to the mob, everyone was profoundly thankful for the presence of the Sikhs (even those who were most eloquently contemptuous of the Italian reliance on native troops), but at the time, when everything was surprisingly well controlled and there was still a disposition among newcomers to believe what the Abyssinians told them, the arrival of a guard of unknown dimensions and the creation, it was believed, of an armed stronghold at the British Legation, seemed to be a slight on the Imperial hospitality which earned the nickname of " Barton's Folly." How wrong we were!

The Italian Legation, meanwhile, was in a unique situation, representing a government that, although not at war, had expressed its intention of going to war within a few weeks. The Minister, Count Vinci, had little of the manner of a professional diplomat. He was stocky, cheerful, courageous, friendly and slightly mischievous; he seemed thoroughly to enjoy his precarious position. He rode out daily into the town, alone or in the company of a single groom. His enemies said that he was seeking to provoke an 'incident.' He entertained liberally, and at his table there was an atmosphere of ease and humour lacking elsewhere in Addis. He was surrounded by spies, both his own and those of the government. For months now the secret police had instituted a surveillance, which came very near to persecution, of his native servants. In Addis and at the provincial consulates they were frequently arrested on one charge or another, questioned and often held in chains. Vinci cheerfully entered his claims for explanation at the Foreign Office, in the certainty that they would receive no attention. Every day he or the first secretary went to the little Fascist club they had formed in the bazaar quarter and sat alone, receiving anyone who cared to interview him. He and his suite still appeared conspicuously at the public functions. As far as he was concerned, negotiations with the Emperor were at an end. Any settlement there might be, would be made in Europe. His immediate business was to maintain the dignity of the future conquerors and to get his nationals out of the country before the trouble started. His only anxiety was the safety of the provincial consuls. There were five regular consulates—at Adowa, Gondar, Harar, Dessye and Debra Markos—and a commercial agency at Magalo. At most of these there were two or three Europeans—a dispenser, wireless operator, besides the normal officials—and a small native guard, sometimes of local troops, sometimes of Italian Eritrean subjects. At this season their journey to the frontier might take several weeks. On September 7 Vinci applied to the Ethiopian Foreign Office for their permission to withdraw. The permission was neither refused nor given; to travel without it, even in normal times, would have been highly dangerous. Belatingetta Herui, the Foreign Minister, prevaricated, maintaining that the consuls must come to Addis, not travel directly, and more conveniently, to the frontier. He did not wish them to have the opportunity of seeing the Ethiopian concentrations of troops and frontier defences. On September 18 Vinci declared that if he did not receive the permission at once, he would instruct his consuls to start their journey without it, and that the Abyssinians must take responsibility for any 'incident' that might occur. It was not until September 22 that facilities were at length given. It was for this reason that two of the consuls were still on the road at the time of the bombardment of Adowa.

The news of the British naval concentration in

the Mediterranean, which convulsed Europe, made little impression in Addis. The single outside event which caused much discussion was the decision of the Committee of Five. Their recommendations reached the Emperor on September 19. He was entertaining the Press to dinner that evening and we expected that some statement might be made on the subject. It was clear, as soon as the terms became known, that they offered no satisfactory solution but that they strengthened the position which the Emperor had adopted of scrupulous legality and devotion to League principles. They recognised and satisfied Italy's complaint that Ethiopia was a bad neighbour; they provided for extensive reforms under European advice, a regular budget, economic development, a national police system. They represented, in fact, the avowed programme of the *Jeunesse d'Ethiopie*. There were two grave objections to them. They offered Italy nothing. The Emperor was to be free to choose his own European advisers, and it was perfectly evident that, after the antagonism inflamed by the events of the preceding months, none of these would be Italian. The rectifications of frontier suggested were valueless, particularly if they were made as compensation for a corridor to the coast, which would deflect trade from the routes which the Italians were seeking to establish through their own territory. After the demonstrative preparations which had been made, the acceptance of these recommendations by Italy would have been a humiliating withdrawal in the face of threatened coercion. The second objection was that the solution they offered to Ethiopia's internal disorder would not have worked in practice. The predominant class— and, I believe, a fair number of the *Jeunesse d'Ethiopie* themselves—would have believed that they had achieved a diplomatic triumph; danger was averted; the new Geneva ju-ju had worked; the white man was tricked again. They would have settled back complacently into their traditional manner of life. The new commissioners would have found themselves frustrated at every turn. The only white men with whom the Ethiopians worked harmoniously were Levantine adventurers. The single Englishman —a man of high principles, experience and notable tact—who had held an advisory post among them found his position untenable and had resigned. If the new advisers were conscientious men they would sooner or later have been obliged to invite armed intervention, in which case a mandate would have to be given to one or other of the Powers, or, at the worst, to a condominium of more than one (an experiment by the League which is proving disastrous in the Pacific). An unconquered Abyssinia would never accept effective reform.

Nothing was said about the proposals at the Emperor's banquet, but it was an interesting evening. It was the first time that I had been inside the new Gibbi, which the Emperor had recently built on the outskirts of the city. The old Gibbi of Menelik, still used for many court functions and for the officers of the personal staff, was the centre of the Imperial rule. This was a private residence, designed especially for the entertainment of Europeans. The old Gibbi had character. It was ramshackle and without plan; a central, semi-European, stone hall, surrounded by a great village of sheds and huts, timber and tin and thatch, with a chapel, a mausoleum, a slaughter-house, barracks and prisons, courts of justice, huge, irregular parade grounds, cages of lions, stables jumbled together on the stockaded hillside. The new Gibbi was like the villa of a retired Midland magnate. It had been furnished and arranged throughout by a firm of London decorators. They had laid the linoleum and displayed the silver-framed photographs. Nothing had been done to add the smallest personal touch.

The footmen wore European liveries. Until a few days before there had been a Swiss chef, but the Abyssinians, even those most eloquent in their desire to suppress slavery, could never accustom themselves to the practice of paying their servants. Having received no wages for many months, the chef gave notice and set up for himself in a little pension-restaurant in the town. The Emperor summoned him back for the Press banquet; he refused to come, so they arrested his entire domestic staff. Still he would not come, so the dinner was provided, I believe, by the ruthless Mr. Kakophilos.

The electric light failed seven times in the course of the evening. This mischance was attributed to M. Idot, who had been observed mingling furtively among the guests. It was said that the Emperor had intended to give a cinema show after dinner and M. Idot wanted to deflect his guests to the *Perroquet*. In this he was certainly successful. It was a rowdy night both there and at Mme. Moriatis's.

The Emperor made other attempts to relieve the tedium of our vigil. The displays of modernity which had formed one of the lighter elements of the coronation were once more revived. We woke up one morning to find the town placarded with trilingual proclamations against cruelty to animals. ' *Considering*,' the English version read, ' *that cruelty and ill-treatment against tamed and utile animals are incompatible with human dignity, the Municipality informs the public that it is formally forbidden to ill-treat animals.*'

A few days later a model prison was opened. This project had captivated the Imperial imagination some years before; plans had been got out by a Swiss contractor and foundations laid; then, as on most Ethiopian undertakings, work had ceased. Now, with a hundred inquisitive foreigners in the town, it was resumed with feverish activity.

There were several existing less ambitious prisons in Addis from which European visitors are rigorously excluded. Minor malefactors, hopping cheerfully about in chains and collecting the money for their release by begging, were a common sight in the country, but an attempt had been made in Addis to keep them out of sight of the photographers, who had a way of sending home their pictures labelled ' Slaves on the way to market.'

On my previous visit I had got inside the prison at Harar. Later, an Italian agent with a camera had done the same, and the results provided several pages in the Geneva dossier and the various pamphlets issued by the Ministry of Propaganda in Rome. The result was not an improvement in the prison but, in future, its absolute inaccessibility to white investigators. It was an appalling spectacle. I am told that the crates in which they confine Manchurian criminals are more disagreeable still, but the Harar gaol remains in my memory as the lowest pit of human misery to which I have ever penetrated. The prisoners were mostly there in discharge of small debts; three or four deaths occurred weekly, I was informed, from typhus. The cells were little hutches built round an open yard, as foul as human habitation could make it. Three or four men were tethered to the wall of each cell, by chains just long enough to allow of their crawling into the open. (It was also common—though I did not see an example myself—for prisoners to be manacled wrist-to-ankle, and left doubled up for months at a time.) They were provided with no food except what their relatives chose to provide. They had no occupation of any kind, but squatted day after day, sick or well, quite hopeless.

The Emperor's new prison offered a standard of comfort not only immeasurably superior to the homes of his law-abiding subjects, but also to most of the Addis hotels. There were shower baths and a laundry, a recreation-room provided with educational works, a dining-room with benches and tables set with enamel ware. Each bunk was provided with a pyjama suit, which was, I believe, sent back to the stores from which it had been borrowed immediately after the official opening.

This took place in the last week in September, on the first fine day we had seen. The sun shone brilliantly on the new concrete; the clouds had lifted and a vast panorama of rolling downland, of blue hill-tops, each crowned with a farm or conical church, and of deep green valleys, was suddenly revealed. The new prison lay at a little distance from the city; we drove to it through fields of new yellow flowers. The Legations, the Press, the photographers, the whole white population, the general staff and the Court were all present. As Vinci walked round behind the Emperor, someone remarked that he was choosing his cell.

The Governorship of the prison was conferred upon one of the progressive, already fully employed, young clerks of the *Jeunesse d'Ethiopie*. We asked him about its future use. Perhaps wishing to enhance its importance, he said it was for the punishment of murderers and high-born rebels. When the last visitor had driven away the gates were locked, a handful of soldiers left on guard, and for the remainder of Haile Selassie's brief reign the place was deserted and forgotten; reports and photographs of the Emperor's enlightened innovation flooded the European and American press ; it had done its work. Malefactors were still expeditiously hustled off to the old, secret prisons.

The more impressive celebrations were those which formed a part of the traditional calendar and had not been specially planned for the edification of the journalists. There was the New Year's day, already mentioned, a domestic feast, for which each household made a little bonfire in the mud outside its doors and danced at nightfall in the rain, clapping, stamping and chanting a monotonous African song. For two days before the whole town became a meat market. They were slaughtering at every corner and the children ran about the streets carrying handfuls of fresh entrails. The rich ate beef and entertained their followers; the poor had mutton. Everyone seemed to be carrying a lamb across his shoulders, or pushing a sheep, wheelbarrow fashion on its fore legs. A series of banquets was given daily at the Palace—the traditional entertainment of the troops and their chiefs, raw beef, red peppers and *tedj*—but no Europeans were allowed to enter, in the ingenuous apprehension that the exhibition of table manners might shock them and undermine the impression created by the new prison and the humane ordinance of the municipality against ill-treating animals.

September 28 was the feast of Maskal, preceded a week earlier by the Emperor's Maskal, and on the day before by a great military review. The origins of this feast are lost in somewhat speculative folk-lore. It is the Spring festival which marks, or is designed to mark, the end of the rains. Its essential feature is the setting up on the eve, and the burning at dawn next day, of the Maskal staff, identical, presumably, with the European maypole. Since the conversion of the country, the day has been Christianised, and the pole is taken to represent the wood of the cross. It is, of course, a purely Abyssinian festival, in which the Moderns and Pagans have no share. It was observed all over the Empire, wherever there was an Abyssinian garrison, and with particular pomp in Addis Ababa.

The ceremony a week before was a personal religious function of the Emperor's, attended by the Court, the Legations and, at this final celebration, by the Press. It was remarkable as the first time that Vinci and the Emperor had met since Vinci's refusal, after an anti-Italian speech of the Emperor's, to attend his birthday reception in July. In some quarters his presence that morning was taken as an augury of peaceful settlement.

The occasion gave the special correspondents the chance, for which their editors had long been waiting, to compose some ' good colorful stuff ' of the kind which had been used so extravagantly during the coronation. What was more surprising was that many of them seemed genuinely impressed by what they saw.

The ceremony took place in the old Gibbi in a great shed, not unlike an aeroplane hangar, where the raw beef banquets were normally held. The room was lit by windows from which were peeling patches of gelatine, in coloured patterns counterfeiting stained glass. Petrol cans, painted pale green, held ragged little palms. At the far end was a great, gilt, canopied divan-throne, in the style which once graced the old Alhambra Music Hall. Here the Emperor sat, with two great bundles of drapery, the Abuna and the Abyssinian prelate, on either side of him. The three were dignified and impressive; two pet dogs sniffed and scratched at their feet. Nosegays of wild flowers were distributed to the waiting assembly. Glittering bunches of priests and deacons began to assemble. The camera was kind to them, for their robes at close quarters were of the shoddiest material—gaudy Japanese vegetable silks, embroidered with sequins and tinsel; there were gilt crowns and bright umbrellas. Presently they formed themselves into a double row and began to dance a kind of clumsy and rather lugubrious Sir Roger de Coverley, swaying from side to side and slowly waving their silver-headed prayer sticks. There was a jingle of silver sistrums and a rhythmic hand drumming, a prolonged, nasal chanting. After a time the Abuna rose from his throne and began an address in Arabic, which his interpreter declaimed in stentorian Amharic. It was a homily upon the significance of the Holy Cross. At length, after about an hour, the Emperor and his suite retired and the ecclesiastics came into the open and posed obligingly to the camera men.

It was customary for apologists to liken the coronation of Ethiopia to that of medieval Europe; there were close parallels, of a kind, to be drawn between Ethiopia, with its unstable but half-sacred monarchy, the feudal fiefs and the frequent insurrections, the lepers and serfs, the chained and tortured captives, the isolation and ignorance, the slow *tempo*, and our own high and chivalrous origins; parallels so close that many humane people accepted them as identical. On this particular morning of the Emperor's Maskal the comparison seemed to be fruitful. We had seen the highest expression of historic Abyssinian culture; this was the Church's most splendid and solemn occasion, in the heart of the Imperial Court. It was natural to consider, as one drove back to one's typewriter, what a ceremony of the kind was like in medieval Europe; of the avenues of fluted columns, branching high overhead into groined and painted roof, each boss and capital a triumph of delicate sculpture, the sweet, precise music, the embroidered vestments, the stained and leaded windows to which later artists look, hopeless of emulation, the learning and austerity of the monastic orders, the royal dignity of the great Churchmen, of a culture which had created an object of delicate and individual beauty for every simple use; metal, stone, ivory and wood worked in a tradition of craftsmanship which makes succeeding generations complete for their humblest product. It was significant to turn from that to the artificial silk and painted petrol cans of Addis Ababa.

A week later, on the eve of Maskal proper, was held the last annual review of the Imperial Guard. This, like the guard itself, was the innovation of Haile Selassie's, which happily reconciled the traditional ceremony of setting up the Maskal pole with the new order.

It took place in the circular space where the Menelik memorial stood, in front of Giorgis. A grandstand had been erected in the inevitable decorative scheme of corrugated iron and artificial silk. The Maskal was planted early in the day by the municipal authorities, without any particular ceremony. It was a tall post, crowned at the summit with a bunch of wild flowers. In a burst of belated energy gangs of workmen were employed, almost until the moment of the Emperor's arrival, patching the worst fissures in the rough pavement. The bazaar was closed for the festival. Dense crowds of peasants had been thronging the streets since dawn. The irregular troops of the immediate neighbourhood had assembled under their chiefs to take part in the display. Many of them carried wands, in the traditional fashion, to cast at the foot of the Maskal.

The ceremony was planned to start soon after midday. There was no knowing how long it would last. The morning was clear and sunny and the majority of the journalists preferred to get their day's work done before proceeding to the show. They typed out expansive descriptions, deposited them at the wireless bureau and took their places in a shelter provided for them at the side of the Imperial stand. Mr. Prospero and the other cinema men had set up their apparatus under the statue of Menelik. The diplomatic corps began to arrive; Vinci and all his suite once again in attendance.

A tremor of anxiety passed through the journalists' stand when, shortly before the Emperor's arrival, the sky became suddenly overcast and an intensely cold wind stirred the gaudy draperies. At one o'clock it began to rain, then to thunder, then to hail. It was the heaviest and longest storm of the season. The whole square was soon submerged. Twenty yards away poor Mr. Prospero was barely visible through the torrent of falling water, pathetically holding a little deer-stalker hat over the lens of his camera.

At half-past one the Emperor arrived in field

uniform accompanied by an escort of sodden lancers. He took his place on the throne and sat immobile, staring into the rain. It was already evident that the roof over our heads was designed more for ornament than protection; water poured in from numerous multiplying and widening holes. A few journalists had brought their typewriters with them. They attempted to write their copy, but the paper turned to pulp under the keys. Still nothing happened. It was necessary for the Abuna to inaugurate the ceremony by walking three times round the Maskal; nothing would induce him— an elderly, infirm man, born in a happier climate— to leave the dry spot his deacons had found for him in the shelter. (Next day it was officially announced in his name—since he himself was unable to leave his bed—that rain on Maskal day, though unusual, was the happiest possible augury for Abyssinian prosperity.)

The tedium of waiting was relieved by a vigorous but losing battle waged by the police against a soaking and very uncompanionable rabble of poor whites, half-castes and Indians, who began filtering over the railings into the Press stand. Every half-hour or so Mr. David, at our earnest request, would push his way in with a posse of police and denounce the gate-crashers. They would be pushed outside into the hail, protesting vehemently in Greek, Armenian, Amharic and French, and, as soon as his back was turned, come clambering back. It was not much drier inside than out, but their racial pride was involved in the struggle.

At last, at quarter-past three, the rain slackened perceptibly. The Abuna emerged, and, with a dejected air, walked round the Maskal, casting a wand at its base. The Emperor and his younger son, the Duke of Harar, followed. Then, as the downpour again increased in violence, the parade began.

The troops varied in character from the Imperial Guard, uniformed, shaven, tolerably smart, to the irregular feudal levies. Both these were impressive. Between them in degree of training were the new volunteers whom we had seen drilling in the street. These struck an unhappy compromise; some of them had uniforms, but none had yet acquired the carriage of regular soldiers. There was nothing at all ridiculous about the totally undisciplined little companies, who cheered and stumbled and chattered and jostled round their chiefs; but the volunteers, laboriously attempting to keep the step, with their caps at odd angles, and expressions on their faces of extreme self-consciousness, made a very silly show.

The procession was arranged in alternate bodies of disciplined and undisciplined troops, ending with the very smart cavalry regiment of the Imperial Guard and sixteen motor lorries carrying anti-aircraft machine guns. This arrangement fulfilled a double purpose; it emphasised for the benefit of his own people and the European visitors the difference between the Imperial Guard and the feudal levies, giving a sample of the change which the new régime hoped to effect universally throughout the Empire, and it separated the wilder men from rival companies with whom they might have come into conflict.

The high spirits of the troops seemed unaffected by the weather. In the coming weeks, as the provincial armies passed through the capital on their way to the Northern front, we were to see several such displays. For most of the Press it was then a new experience. The old chiefs, almost without exception, looked superb. Their gala costume varied in magnificence with their wealth. They had headdresses and capes of lion skin, circular shields and extravagantly long, curved swords, decorated with metal and coloured stuff; their saddles and harness were brilliant and elaborate. Examined in detail, of course, the ornaments were of wretched quality, the work of Levantine craftsmen in the Addis bazaar, new, aiming only at maximum ostentation for a minimum price; there was nothing which bore comparison with the splendour of a North African or Asiatic workmanship. But in their general effect, as they emerged from the watery haze which enclosed us, strutted and boasted before the Emperor, and were hustled away in the middle of their speeches by the Court Chamberlains, those old warriors were magnificent.

Boasting was a particular feature of all these

parades. Sometimes it was done by special minstrels, sometimes by the chief himself, who would spur his mule up to the steps of the throne, rein it back on its haunches, brandish his spear and recite the deeds of bloodshed he had achieved in the past and those he proposed to do in the future; sometimes he would dismount and dance before the Emperor with drawn sword, chanting of his prowess. If he were allowed to continue too long in this manner he intoxicated himself and in a kind of ecstasy, sword whirling, eyes turned up, beard and lips spattered with foam, would constitute a serious danger to those near him. (When the Kambata army came through they cut open the head of one of the chamberlains in their enthusiasm.) The greater part of these recitations, my interpreter told me, dealt with the first battle of Adowa; most of the promises of future service were taunts at Italy. Vinci and his staff sat through the wet afternoon listening with polite, if slightly ironical, attention.

An incongruous and more sombre note was struck by the sudden appearance among these flamboyant demonstrators of a bedraggled little procession of shivering school-children, who sang a hymn in quavering, barely audible tones.

The journalists meanwhile were beginning to slip away to the wireless bureau to send, at urgent rates, contradictions of their earlier messages. Still the procession went on. It ended, shortly before sunset, with four Red Cross vans. Perhaps they were appropriate to the last festival of free Abyssinia.

Another week followed, full of whispered rumours; more journalists and cinema men arrived. I bought a petulant and humorless baboon which lived in my room at the Deutsches Haus, and added very little to the interest of these dull days. There were rowdy evenings at *Le Secret* and the *Perroquet*. The Spaniard went back to resume his duties in Paris. Patrick and I gave a dinner-party in his honour, which was overclouded for him by the loss of his sixpenny fountain-pen. "Who of you has taken my feather?" he kept asking with great earnestness. "I cannot work without my feather."

At last, on October 2, came the announcement which had been so often predicted, that general mobilisation would be proclaimed on the morrow. It was preceded by the formal complaint that Ethiopian territory had been violated at Mount Moussa Ali, south-west of Assab on the borders of French Somaliland. An Italian force, as Wazir Ali Beg had reported a month earlier, had established a base on the Ethiopian side of the frontier. Notices were posted inviting the Press to attend ' a ceremony of great importance ' which was to be held next day at the old Gibbi. Everybody knew what that meant.

I drove to the Italian Legation, but found them all in a fever of activity. Presumably they had already received news from Eritrea that the war was about to start. It was particularly gay that evening in the bars. Next morning we all assembled at the Palace at half-past ten. We were shown straight into an airless gallery and kept there. I remember saying to the Reuter's correspondent, "Well, now that they *have* at last mobilised, I suppose —— and —— (naming two abnormally untruthful colleagues who had anticipated the morning's order by ten days) will have to start announcing the bombardment of Adowa."

No one knew quite what to expect, and even the most daring of the journalists had decided to wait and see what happened before composing their reports. Various almost liturgical ceremonies were expected; we were told in some quarters that the Emperor would set up his standard in person; that his crimson tent would be pitched as a rallying point for the armies; that the great drum of Menelik would be beaten, which had not sounded since 1895.

The drum was there; we could hear it clearly from our place of confinement, beating a series of single thuds, slow as a tolling bell. When eventually the doors were thrown open and we emerged on to the terrace, we saw the drum, a large ox-hide stretched over a wooden bowl. It may or may not have belonged to Menelik; all the whites said that it had and Mr. David politely agreed.

A flight of stone steps led from the terrace to the parade ground, where a large, but not very large, crowd had assembled. They were all men. Over his shoulder I watched an American journalist typing out a description of the women under their mushroom-like umbrellas. There were no women and no umbrellas; merely a lot of black fuzzy heads and white cotton clothes. The Palace police were trying to keep the crowd back, but they pushed forward until only a small clearing remained, immediately below the steps. Here Mr. Prospero and half a dozen of his colleagues were grinding away behind tripods.

The drum stopped and the people were completely silent as the Grand Chamberlain read the decree. It took some time. He read it very loudly and clearly. At the end there were three concerted bursts of clapping. Then the men made a rush for the Palace; it was unexpected and spontaneous. They wanted to see the Emperor. Most of them had swords or rifles. They flourished these wildly and bore down upon the little group of photographers, who, half fearing a massacre, scuttled for safety, dragging along their cumbrous apparatus as best they could. The crowd caught poor Mr. Prospero. knocked him down and kicked him about, not in any vindictive spirit, but simply because he was in the way. One of them eventually put him on his feet, laughing, but not before he had sustained some sharp injuries.

Upstairs the decree, in quite different terms, we found later, was being read to the journalists in French by Dr. Lorenzo. He could not make himself heard above the shouting. He stood on a chair, a diminutive, neat, black figure, crying for attention.

149

A great deal of noise came from the journalists themselves. I had seldom seen them to worse advantage. Dr. Lorenzo had in his hand a sheaf of copies of the decree. The journalists did not want to hear him read it. They wanted to secure their copies and race with them for the wireless bureau. Lorenzo kept crying in French, " Gentlemen, gentlemen, I have something of great importance to communicate to you."

He held the papers above his head and the journalists jumped for them, trying to snatch, like badly brought up children at a Christmas party.

The soldiers had now worked themselves into high excitement and were streaming past, roaring at the top of their voices.

Lorenzo led a dozen of us into the Palace, where in comparatively good order he was able to make his second announcement. He was clearly in a state of deep emotion himself; the little black hands below the starched white cuffs trembled. " His Majesty has this morning received a telegram from Ras Seyoum in the Tigre," he said. " At dawn this morning four Italian war planes flew over Adowa and Adigrat. They dropped seventy-eight bombs, causing great loss of life among the civilian population. The first bomb destroyed the hospital at Adowa, where many women and children had taken refuge. At the same time Italian troops invaded the Province of Agame, where a battle is now raging."

V

ANTICLIMAX

I

THE excitement barely survived the transmission of our cables. By afternoon the cheering crowd had melted away and was dozing silently in their tukals. Shutters were put up on the Greek-Italian grocery store and a guard posted before it, while at the back door journalists competed with the French Legation to buy the last tins of caviare. There were guards at the Italian Legation, the Italian Hospital and mission, the house of the military attaché; these buildings were out of bounds to Ethiopians and, for all practical purposes, to ourselves, for the soldiers in charge were a surly lot; Mr. David at the Press Bureau assured us that the guards were there merely for the protection of the Italians, that we had only to show our Press cards to obtain admission; in fact for the first day or two we were turned back in the most uncompromising manner; later their vigilance became milder and Vinci and his staff even accepted invitations to dinner.

His position was to become increasingly anomalous. It had been odd during the preceding month; now that hostilities had actually begun, it was without precedent. The Emperor was reluctant to order his withdrawal, for fear of compromising the posture he had assumed of quaker-like patience. No one knew the exact extent or purpose of the hostilities. Some said the bombardment of Adowa was a local reprisal for the deflection by the Abyssinians of a stream flowing to the Italian lines. No one knew how abruptly or effectively the League of Nations might intervene. In those days of early October, in Addis Ababa at least, it was thought possible that there might be some concerted, exemplary action which would smother the newborn war almost before it had taken independent breath. It was important to keep means of communication open with the enemy. So, for the time being, Vinci stayed on, attended by a somewhat incongruous entourage of nuns and grocers. He had deserved a holiday and he was enjoying it. For four years he had been at an arduous, responsible and unpleasant post, trying to maintain a working method which with each year had been more obviously futile; a routine of constant insult, constant protest, constant evasion; always hampered by the jealousies of his European colleagues. Now the make-believe was over; the uniforms and evening clothes were packed; the journalists who had pestered him were at a distance. With Latin relish he settled down to a few days of leisure.

ANTICLIMAX

That afternoon and evening we drove round the town in search of ' incidents,' but everything was profoundly quiet. News of the bombardment of Adowa was now all over the bazaars, but it seemed to cause little stir. It would be impertinent to attempt any certain definition of what the people felt. Perhaps the majority of them believed that the war had already been in progress for some time. Adowa was a very long way off. Practically no one in Addis had ever been there. It was known to them by name, as the place where the white men had been so gloriously cut to pieces forty years before. It was inhabited by Tigreans, a people for whom they had little liking. News of its destruction was received in Addis rather as we, in London, read of floods in China or earthquakes in Japan. There seemed a complete absence of indignation, an absence of all emotion except a mild sporting enthusiasm at the prospect of a good season's shooting.

The Europeans, Levantines and Americans, on the other hand, fell into a cold sweat of terror. The Emperor's American adviser had at this time organised a daily tea party of specially sympathetic correspondents, to whom he divulged the government communiqués a day before they were officially issued. This group became a centre from which Ethiopian propaganda radiated. On the afternoon of October 3, ' the Leaker,' as he was familiarly known, gave it out that an air raid was expected on

Addis that evening. The effect was galvanic. One group of American journalists hastily concluded a deal for the lease of a mansion immediately next door to the Italian Legation. They packed up their stores and luggage and their accumulations of trashy souvenirs and set off in secrecy to their new home. Unfortunately they were contravening a municipal bye-law which forbade a change of address without previous permission. I cannot help suspecting that Mr. Kakophilos must have tipped off the police; there was a touch of saturnine triumph in the air with which he welcomed their return, an hour later, under guard, to his hotel. A similar fate befell a neurotic young Canadian who set out to hide on the top of Mount Entoto. Other journalists took refuge in outlying missions and hospitals, or shared their bedrooms with their chauffeurs for fear that, when the alarm came, they might find their cars usurped by black women and children. Others are said to have sat up all night playing stud poker in gas masks. Timidity was infectious. A passing motor bicycle would have us all at the window staring skywards. A few hardened topers remained sober that evening for fear of sleeping too heavily. But the night passed undisturbed by any except the normal sounds —the contending loud-speakers of the two cinemas, the hyaenas howling in the cemetery. Few of us slept well. The first two hours after dawn were the most likely time for a raid, but the sun—at last it was full summer—brought reassurance. After a slightly strained week-end we settled down to our former routine. On Monday night there was a bacchanalian scene at Mme. Idot's, where, among other songs of international popularity, ' Giovanezza ' was sung in a litter of upturned tables and broken crockery.

2

From now until the very end—and, indeed, long after the end—the one department of the Ethiopian government which worked with tolerable efficiency was the propaganda. Its aim, as is usual, was to represent the enemy as both ruthless and ineffective. Mass disloyalty, cowardice, extreme physical weakness and cruelty were the characteristics imputed to the invading armies; restraint, courage, wisdom and uniform success of the defenders; women, children and the medical services the chief victims. These are the normal objectives of a propagandist campaign in time of war; the Ethiopians pursued them tolerably well.

First there were the public utterances of the Emperor. These were drafted for him by his professional white advisers, but it is probable that he took a large share in their composition. They were designed entirely for foreign consumption and were quite admirable. They were repeated throughout the world and more than any single feature of the situation stirred the women, clergy and youths of the civilised races, conservative and socialist alike, to that deep, cordial, altruistic and absolutely ineffective sympathy which has been his reward.

Besides these, the government issued occasional bulletins of news. They were, naturally enough, incomplete and tendencious, but, at first, as far as they went, surprisingly truthful. When they proved false it was generally because the local commanders were lying, not the central government. News of reverses was delayed and suppressed, casualties among the fighting forces minimised and those among non-combatants exaggerated, but I do not know of a case in which the truth was officially denied or a lie categorically affirmed. The bulletins compared very favourably with those issued by any nation in time of war.

It is worth noticing one change of policy among the propagandists. In the early stages of the war, so long, in fact, as the Abyssinian armies appeared to be holding out successfully, attention was constantly called to the desertions of Italian native troops. These were represented as mutinous and eager for revenge against the oppression of their masters. Later, when the break-up of the Abyssinian defence was apparent, a new line was adopted and the myth propagated, and eagerly received in England, that the Italians owed their victory entirely to native soldiers while they themselves remained at a safe distance. Ras Kassa went so far as to give public utterance to the statement that no white troops at all had appeared in the front line. It was a double-edged argument, for, if a measure were needed to judge the relative merits of Abyssinian and Italian imperialism, there could be no more certain one than the subject people's willingness to die for the régime. The Ethiopian subject races revolted at the first opportunity and finally drove the Emperor from the country; the Eritreans followed their white officers with ferocious devotion.

The real work of the propaganda department was done through unofficial channels. To the horde of competing journalists the government communiqués were of negligible importance. They were transmitted instantly in full by Reuter's and the other agencies and gave no material for the special news which the editors were demanding. This had to be procured by other means; it had to be jealously guarded from rivals. It could not be investigated for fear of attracting their attention. An exclusive lie was more valuable than a truth which was shared with others.

A point of this kind was particularly apt for Ethiopian intelligence; it exemplified just what they had always thought about Europeans—an unscrupulous, impatient, avaricious, credulous people —and they exploited it to the full. They worked partly by means of unofficial revelations—usually in hints or guarded agreement with the statements which their interviewer was attempting to impose on them—in official quarters; partly in the employment of foreigners and servants to spread news which they wanted to have believed. The information was given to the journalists singly, so that each imagining himself especially astute or especially privileged, gave it corresponding prominence in his despatch. An example occurred during the first days of the war in the case of the hospital at Adowa.

The first communiqué, read in dramatic circumstances by Dr. Lorenzo, asserted that the first bomb of the attack had fallen on ' the hospital,' destroying it and killing many women and children. The statement was, presumably, taken from Ras Seyoum's despatch and passed on directly to us and to Geneva without enquiry. When we began to look for details, our doubts were aroused whether there had ever been a hospital there at all. No such thing existed as a native hospital; no Red Cross units had yet appeared in the field; the medical work of the country was entirely in mission hands, either of Catholic orders—Capucins, Lazarists, Consolata—or Swedish and American Protestants. The headquarters of these organisations knew nothing about a hospital at Adowa, nor did the Consulates know of any of their nationals engaged there. The publication of the news was already having the desired effect in Europe; a letter, which caused great amusement when it reached us, appeared in *The Times* expressing the hope that '' the noble nurses had not died in vain,'' but at Addis Ababa suspicions

158

were aroused that our legs were being pulled. Mr. David and Dr. Lorenzo, when pressed, had to admit that they knew no more than was disclosed in the first bulletin; there *had been* a hospital—it was now destroyed, they maintained stoutly, and added that it was clearly marked with the red cross; apart from that they had no information.

But suddenly, from other sources, a flood of detail began to reach us. There was an Abyssinian servant who had been treated there two years ago for a pain in his leg by a great number of American doctors and nurses; the hospital was a fine building in the centre of the town.

There was a Greek who knew the place well. It was managed by Swedes and lay at a short distance along the Adigrat road.

There was a Swiss architect and government contractor—a jolly fellow, married to a half-caste; he was responsible for most of the ugliest of the recent public buildings—who was able to give Patrick confidential but absolutely authentic information about the nurse who had been killed; she was of Swedish birth but American nationality; she had been blown to bits. He had heard all about it on the telephone from a friend on the spot.

The most circumstantial story came from an American negro who was employed as aviator by the Ethiopian government. I met him at his tailor's on the Saturday morning, ordering a fine new uniform. He had been at Adowa, he claimed, at the time of the bombardment. More than this, he had been in the hospital. More than this, he had been drinking cocoa with the nurse five minutes before her death. She was a handsome lady, thirty-two years old, five foot five in height. They had been sitting in the hospital—clearly marked by the red cross—when the first bomb had fallen. The airman's first thought, he said, was for the safety of his machine, which was lying a mile outside the town. Except for himself and the doctor there were no other men in the town. It was populated solely by women and children. He had lain near his aeroplane for some hours while the bombs fell. The Italians had flown very badly, he said, and bombed most erratically (" Mr. Waugh, do you realise, *I* might have been killed *myself*? "). Eventually he had returned to see the place demolished and the nurse dead. He had then flown back to Addis, where the Emperor had been deeply moved by his story.

When we pointed out to the Press Bureau that neither the Swedish nor American consuls knew of the hospital, Mr. David had an ingenious explanation. It was true, he said, that the nurses and doctor had not passed through Addis Ababa and registered there; they had entered the country from Eritrea, whence they had been driven by Italian brutality.

Cables were soon arriving from London and New York: ' *Require earliest name life story photograph American nurse upblown Adowa.*' We replied ' *Nurse*

unupblown,' and after a few days she disappeared from
the news. Later, when the Ethiopian government
made its comprehensive complaint on the acts
against international convention committed by
Italian airmen, the Adowa hospital was not mentioned. Its brief vogue, however, was of assistance
to one thoroughly deserving Englishman.

Captain P. had arrived some time before and had
been having a typically trying time. He was the
officer sent in advance by the British Ambulance,
voluntarily subscribed and equipped in London for
service on the Abyssinian front. His job was to
arrange for the arrival of the unit and he came in
the expectation of a cordial reception. As the
American doctor had found, enthusiasm for the Red
Cross was not strong in Abyssinia. News that a
subscription had been opened in England was
warmly received, but there had been a marked
abatement when it was learned that Englishmen
intended to come and spend it themselves, to go
pushing about behind the lines wasting good money
on men who had been fools enough to get incapaci-
tated; worse still, giving equal attention to wounded
enemies. More than this, the British, very wisely
as events proved, had decided to employ only their
own men. They would bring British native orderlies
from Kenya and work under advice from Addis
Ababa, but as a single, indivisible unit, with their
own commissariat and disciplinary system. The
scum of the Addis missions, flabby-faced, soft-spoken

youths, had already been recruited into an ' Ethiopian Red Cross Corps,' and could be seen lounging and giggling in an empty shop on the main street. The authorities wished Captain P. to take these into his unit instead of the men from Kenya. Negotiations were carried on through the intermediary of the head of one of the missions—a naturalised Ethiopian subject, educated in America, of no defined theological complexion—and were intolerably protracted. Captain P. had come with a pardonable sense of vicarious benefaction. He was greeted with the customary suspicion and delay. On Friday the 4th he was in despair and had delivered his ultimatum that he would leave Addis by the next train unless an agreement was reached. By that evening the Adowa hospital scare was at its height. The Abyssinians suddenly saw the vast possibilities for propaganda in the presence in a dangerous situation of a genuine Red Cross hospital. Their tone changed. Captain P. was informed next day that the British unit would be welcome; indeed, that the Emperor could barely contain his anxiety for its immediate arrival. ' My people are lying wounded in the hills; there is no one to tend them,' he said in a moving speech. So Captain P. set off for Berbera and, rather more than two months later, the gallant ill-starred unit arrived in the country. The ' Ethiopian Red Cross ' continued to hang about the city. Some weeks later they were put in charge of an Indian who had a scheme for reconciling Christianity and Mohamedanism, a very pious American youth who left the table if wine was shown him, and two chatty Irishmen, one a doctor, the other a publican, who were embarrassed by no such fad. This corps added one more to the many bright elements of the campaign. It was constantly being ordered to the front, but evening after evening the familiar faces were to be seen in the Addis bars. By the beginning of December they had got to Dessye, where half of the native orderlies were under treatment for venereal disease; others were in chains for breaches of discipline; others were in tears at the prospect of moving nearer the fighting. There were disagreements among the officers, and they occupied separate quarters. After it was all over one of our most august papers conveyed the idea that they had been in the front line from the beginning of the war.

3

News of the capture of Adowa and Adigrat reached us on October 7, long after its publication to the rest of the world. It caused little stir, for the defence of the two towns had never been part of the Abyssinian strategy. The advance appeared to have been held up for three days by scouts and skirmishers. We had all expected a sensationally rapid penetration from north and south. In the Ogaden rain was said to be still falling. There had been bombing there, but, it was reported, barely two out of three bombs exploded; they splashed harmlessly into the mud. Incendiary bombs were extinguished or fizzled like damp fireworks in the marshes. The soldiers, when they spoke of aeroplanes, used feminine suffixes—a grammatical form expressive of supreme contempt. It was pointed out that in those clusters of tents and mud huts a bomb was of greater value than anything it could destroy; a house could be rebuilt in a week-end. As the anxiety for our own safety became calmer, we believed that the great attack had in some way gone off at half-cock.

We still believed that the railway was doomed. On Tuesday the 8th ' positively the last ' train left for Djibouti. There was something very like a riot at the station as frantic refugees attempted to board it, and the station police locked out legitimate passengers who had reserved their places. For the first time the scene approximated to the descriptions which, as early as August, had been filling the world's Press. It was now too late to be of interest— another example of the inverted time lag between the event and its publication which marked all our professional efforts in the country. One contrast remains vivid in my memory among the confused impressions of the railway station. A cattle truck packed with soldiers on the way to the southern front; their rifles had been taken away for fear they got into mischief during the journey, but most of them had weapons of a kind; all were in a delirious condition, hoarse, staring, howling for blood. In the next coach sat a dozen Italian nuns on the way to the coast; fresh faced, composed, eyes downcast, quietly telling their beads.

It was not until October 10 that any action was taken with regard to the Italian Legation. The consul and his staff had arrived from Dessye. There was now only the commercial agent from Magalo on the road. Vinci was unwilling to leave without him; the Emperor made an order for his expulsion. It was one of his few injudicious utterances. Instead of basing the order on the indisputable fact that a state of war existed between the two countries, he coupled it with accusations of personal bad faith against the Minister, espionage and abuse of diplomatic privilege. The sequel was the richly comic incident of October 12.

Vinci's departure was announced for eight in the morning. There was to be nothing unobtrusive about it. The Abyssinians were anxious to demonstrate before the world that they were a highly courteous and civilised nation; all, and more than all, the full formalities were to be observed. A printed order was issued the evening before giving the programme for the day. Train and station were prepared for a ceremony of the most dignified nature. A guard of honour of the household cavalry was waiting at dawn outside the Legation gates. By eight o'clock the diplomatic corps were pacing the carpeted platform. Mr. Prospero had erected a platform for his cinema camera. All the photographers were there and all the reporters. Presently the luggage arrived, prominent in its midst a dripping packing case containing bottled beer on ice, and a caged leopard. The Italian consul and the two secretaries were there, looking as though they had been awakened uncommonly early after an uncommonly late night. But of Vinci, or the military attaché, Calderini, there was no sign.

An hour passed. The British, French and American Ministers conferred anxiously. A rumour began to travel along the platform that there had been a hitch. Some of us struggled through the crowd, found a car and drove to the Italian Legation. The squadron of lancers had dismounted and were squatting by their horses. There was also a picket of infantry and a temporary telephone station. No one was allowed inside the gates. A zealous young colonial reporter climbed the wall; was captured and frog-marched, rather roughly, to imprisonment in the telephone hut. We drove back to the station. The train was still there; the luggage and the leopard were on board; the diplomatic corps had gone home to breakfast. The consul's greenish face appeared apprehensively at a carriage window. At half-past ten the train started. At the last moment one of the secretaries jumped out on the off-side and took refuge in an outbuilding. He was disarmed, arrested and sent on later to join the train further down the line.

Back to the Italian Legation. The Ethiopian Foreign Minister was just leaving, alone; a puzzled black face under a bowler hat. He drove to the Belgian Legation to consult the doyen; what did a highly courteous and civilised nation do, when, in time of war, a Minister refused to accept his passport? The doyen did not know.

All the photographers and the cameramen had now assembled outside the gates of the Italian Legation and were picnicking under the hedge. The guards were in a bad temper and there were several scuffles. The colonial had been released and was now alternately protesting and apologising. Inside Vinci and Calderini, having completed a leisurely toilet, took their coffee on the terrace and later settled down to a hand or two of piquet in chancery. All manner of rumours spread through the bazaars: that there was a mine below the Gibbi and Vinci was waiting his moment to press a button and blow it up. David and Lorenzo said, justly, as they had so often said before, that he was ' provoking an incident.'

Vinci and Calderini stayed in Addis for another fortnight. Their attitude was, primarily, that their place was in the country so long as any of their subordinates remained there. Application had been made in good time for the consul's recall. Abyssinian suspicion and obstructiveness had marred the dignified departure that had been planned for them. The order of expulsion had included personal charges; to accept it might be construed as an admission of guilt. But more than these official reasons, there was, I believe, an element of mischief in the matter. As future conquerors, the Italians chose to withdraw their representative, as they had chosen to attack, entirely at their own convenience. They were not going to be hustled out at the command of their future subjects.

They were removed from the Legation and kept in absolute isolation at Ras Desta's house while the Magalo agent made his way slowly—almost imperceptibly—towards the railway line. Repeated messages were sent from the Emperor to hurry him up. He cut down his day's marches to fifteen, then to twelve, finally to ten miles; it was fatiguing, he said, and he enjoyed collecting butterflies on the way. At last he reached Hadama station, where Vinci joined him and they proceeded together to the coast.

During his captivity the Press Bureau did all they could to render Vinci's position ignominious. Lorenzo and his colleagues said that the reason he could not leave was that he was in an alcoholic stupor; he sat all day drooling over the whisky bottle, talking about his ruined career and the pains of hell. A few correspondents loyally cabled the story back, but few of them believed it and, I think, no English newspaper published it. When, eventually, Vinci emerged, spruce and cheerful, it was to go by the quickest route to Mogadishu, where, for the rest of the war, he commanded a company of native infantry with conspicuous success.

4

Provincial armies now began to appear in the capital, to do homage to the Emperor on the way to the northern front. The first and most formidable were from Kambata; they had been on the march for ten days or more and arrived lean and defiant. Most of them had never been in the city before; they swaggered through the traffic and caused trouble to anyone who obstructed. They threatened the gentle Radical and nearly lynched the two colonials who rode out to their camp to take snapshots; they created some sort of disturbance at the Gibbi, the details of which never came out; a chamberlain was said to have been cut down and several servants injured in the Emperor's presence. They had been told that Ras Seyoum had just retaken Adowa and massacred 30,000 whites, including Mussolini's son. The tale went to their heads. They got very drunk in the *tedj* houses, refused to pay and had several fights with the civic police. Soon they were hustled off to the front without being granted the ceremonial march-past which they expected. Many of them were accompanied by women from their province; squat little negresses padding along beside the column, bowed double under loads of provisions and babies.

The men from Wollaga and Shoa—Ras Moulugetta's own men—were better behaved and were
given their parade. It was like the Maskal review.
The Emperor and his court sat under a canopy while
the men streamed past him, hour after hour. They
came in little knots, each man clinging, if he could,
to his chief's saddle, rushed to the foot of the throne
shouting and dancing and were driven on with canes.
I got my interpreter to take down some of the things
which they shouted:

'*When he was a calf we drove him away with sticks*'
(referring to 1896); '*now he is a fat bull and we will
slaughter him and eat him.*'

'*You have kept us too long. All our enemies are
already slain by the men of the other provinces.*'

'*Never fear, we will please you. We will soon be at
the sea.*'

News of Haile Selassie Gugsa's submission was
suppressed at Addis Ababa until several days after it
was known in Europe; it reached us first as the
rumour that he had tried to desert but had been
shot by his own men; in this form it was held
by the majority of the natives long after a more
truthful version had been issued by the Press
Bureau. But it caused no alarm. It was believed that Kassa's Galla cavalry had invaded
Eritrea and were harassing the Italian communications. There was an atmosphere of highest
optimism everywhere.

ANTICLIMAX

It was rumoured that the Emperor would shortly proceed north and make his headquarters at Dessye; that if he did so the Press would be allowed to go too. Meanwhile we were more than ever starved of credible information. A censorship had been imposed which worked irregularly and capriciously. At first it was put in charge of a very young Belgian— one of the ex-officers who had offered their services to the Abyssinians. He knew very little English and on the first morning contented himself with sending back, without any comment except that they could not be sent, all the cables submitted to him and then closing his office for the day. Later he explained that nothing might be sent which mentioned the Emperor, numbers or movements of troops, war news other than the official communiqués, local news which might be of use to the enemy or which reflected upon the standards of Abyssinian civilisation. No particular details would be expunged; the entire message would be stopped which contained any such offensive matter. This ordinance seemed to impose a complete cessation of all our activities and we received it, either gladly or in a frenzy of rage, according as we valued our jobs. Rage predominated. A special meeting was called of the Foreign Press Association, at which, for the first time, almost the entire Press appeared and apparent solidarity was maintained. A protest was drafted in the most uncompromising terms declaring that until we had attention to our grievances we

would boycott the wireless and that if we did not
receive an answer from the government by the
following evening we would ask to be withdrawn.
We asked for a new censor who had some acquaintance with the languages he dealt in, who kept regular
hours, who would read our cables in our presence
and point out what passages he found objectionable,
who would impose a more reasonable code. We
elected a deputation to wait on Dr. Lorenzo with
our protest and explain it to him. We would
negotiate through this deputation and maintain our
strike until they had come to terms. We parted
in good humour with the prospect of a holiday.
That was at noon. By breakfast time next day a
group of correspondents, including one of the elected
deputies, had opened private negotiations with the
Belgian. From that moment it became clear that
the Foreign Press Association was not going to serve
any useful purpose. No answer was received to our
protest by the time we had specified or for some
days afterwards. When it came it was a blunt
refusal to consider it. Meanwhile everyone went
on working as before. The censor became less
draconian and was later superseded by a scholarly
looking Abyssinian. The Foreign Press Association
met once more, when two Americans challenged one
another to fight and a third was sick. After that it
ceased to exist even in name. The Radical gave the
money that had been collected to the head of the
wireless bureau.

ANTICLIMAX

The camera men were even more unhappily placed than the correspondents. Their apparatus rendered them conspicuous and most of the native soldiers had an exaggerated idea of the value which their portraits might be to the enemy. The cinema companies in particular had invested huge sums in their expeditions and were getting very little in return for it.

Two hundred or more of the Addis Ababa prostitutes appeared one day dressed in high-heeled sandals and ultramarine male uniforms. This was a golden opportunity for the photographers, who got them to pose with rifles and swords and sent back the results entitled ' Abyssinian Amazons. Famous Legion of Fighting Women leave for the Front,' to the great distress of Dr. Lorenzo and Mr. David, who hoped, and eventually succeeded in making good copy out of the casualties among the female camp followers.

One group of cinema men purchased the goodwill of a chief who was encamped with his men in the hills behind Addis and were able to stage some fairly effective charades of active service. Later at Dessye the ' Ethiopian Red Cross ' lent itself to a vivid imposture, staging a scene of their own heroic services under fire, with iodine to counterfeit blood and fireworks and flares for a bombardment. One prominent photographer had brought out with him a set of small bombs which he was able to discharge from his position at the camera by means of an electric cable. He had some difficulty explaining them at the French customs and I do not know if they were ever used. Those who had worked during the Chinese wars—where, it seemed, whole army corps could be hired cheaply by the day and even, at a special price, decimated with real gunfire—complained bitterly of the standard of Abyssinian venality.

The white population of the town pursued their normal routine of petty and profitless trade. Like all my colleagues I now had two or three of them in my employment bringing me wretched scraps of news, mostly about municipal taxation. Mme. Monatis showed signs of despair, spoke daily of a massacre, and tried to persuade her husband to pack up. One evening when she was showing a French version of ' Peg o' my Heart,' her cinema was visited by the picturesque retinue of one of the provincial magnates, who came with women, bodyguard and two half-grown lions who were left on the steps in charge of his slaves. The brief run on the bank came to an end. The thaler went up in value; the engine drivers of the railway did a brisk trade in smuggling silver. Various statesmen and warriors returned from exile and were reconciled to the Emperor. The French population organised itself in a defence corps. Issa tribesmen shot down an Italian aeroplane and hid for days, not knowing if they had done well or ill. An Abyssinian airman came very near being shot down by his fellow-countrymen at Dessye. An Egyptian Prince arrived to establish a Red Crescent hospital. The Yemen Arabs were reported to be active. We eked out our despatches with such small items of news. Already some correspondents began to talk of leaving, and the most distinguished veteran actually left. The rest of us centred all our hopes on the long-deferred trip to Dessye. Various dates—the anniversary of his accession, St. George's Day—were suggested as the time of the Emperor's departure. In the interval of waiting I decided on another visit to Harar.

On our previous journey we found that the further we went from Addis Ababa the milder we found official restrictions; now the case was reversed. Awash, where the train halted for the night, was a military post under the command of a Swiss. A boisterous French adventurer was in charge at Diredawa. We were no longer allowed to sit out after dinner on the hotel verandah; all lights had to be screened. There and at Harar sentries were posted every few yards along the streets and no one was allowed to go out of doors after dark without escort. Charles G. had had the fortune to witness a fight between two of the European police officers. As a result he had lately been expelled on a charge of espionage. His parting act was to buy a slave and give her to Mati Hari as a tip. At Harar the evacuation was almost complete. Few families now slept in the town; most of the stalls in the bazaar were shuttered; those that were open had been deserted by their proprietors and the stock was being sold off by listless underlings. The chief of police, formerly so cordial, now barely troubled himself to acknowledge our greetings. He had taken gravely to the bottle and might be seen daily, from early morning, sunk in gloom, at Mr. Karasselos's hotel, alternately sipping Mr. Karasselos's brandy and giving vent to a nervous, retching cough. The Hararis' brief military enthusiasm was over. There were now no volunteers drilling in the streets. Attempts had been made, with small success, to get them to the front. Now the order was that all Abyssinians were to proceed south and leave the Hararis with the task of garrisoning their city.

The ancient antagonism of cross and crescent seemed at last to have been reconciled; red crosses had sprung up everywhere. There was one on the Emperor's Gibbi, another on the Law Courts, another on the Treasury, another on a little tin shed next to the Belgian orderly-room, another, partly obliterated but still clearly visible, on the roof of the wireless station. Two old-established missions— French and Swedish—maintained a medical service, but there was no ambulance corps of any kind in the city. I sent my interpreter out to try and obtain information about what preparations were being made in these other buildings; he returned unsuccessful. He had been refused admission everywhere; by questioning the guards and friends in the town he learned that it was proposed to put wounded there should any arrive. No special steps had been taken for their accommodation. The shed at the barracks was said to house a small fund of money subscribed locally for humane purposes.

There had been a panic in the city on the day of the bombardment of Adowa. Mr. Karasselos, among others, had prepared for flight and the journalists quartered in his hotel had taken refuge at the British Consulate. They were still encamped there, although Mr. Karasselos had later reopened his door; after two days of sordid discomfort I joined them.

The consul controlled his guests with amiability and tact and, as a result, the acrimonious competition of Addis Ababa hardly existed. The wireless had imposed a limit of fifty words daily on press messages. Every morning the journalists drove into the city and sat with their typewriters in Mr. Karasselos's dining-room; here their various informants brought them the news. At noon they returned to the consulate, lunched heavily and dozed away the rest of the day. Even at this dark hour of its history the gentle atmosphere of Harar exercised a benign influence, shaming the toughest go-getters into temporary leisured decency.

My interpreter—' my name is Mustafa Jimma but gentlemen call me James '—who had been with me now for several weeks, was a ' British-protected person ' from the Soudan—an inestimable advantage, for Ethiopian subjects lived in constant fear of police persecution. He spoke English, Amharic, Arabic and Harari. As a Moslem he enjoyed the confidence of the townspeople; he had lived there some years previously, and still had friends in the place. One day he came to me and said that one of the sheiks of the Mosque wished to talk to me.

The meeting was arranged with the utmost secrecy, in a bedroom at the native inn. I went there first, alone, slipped as unobtrusively as possible from the street into the shady court, and climbed to the gallery. The only inmates were two torpid Arabs, browsing on *khat*. Presently James returned leading a venerable Harari, white-bearded, white-turbaned, white-robed. James had clearly been talking about the importance of his employer. I explained to the old man that I was merely the reporter for a newspaper, but he politely smiled away these subterfuges. He believed that I was an emissary from the British Government and the purpose of his visit was to persuade me, in the name of numerous Moslem elders, to propose the conquest of Harar and its absorption into British Somaliland. Later in the week I had a second interview with him in similar circumstances; on that occasion he brought a friend with him, a cautious old landowner, who had suffered spoliation at Abyssinian hands. We sat in a row on the couch in the little whitewashed cell, while James stood before us and interpreted, fluently and, I believe, quite honestly.

In its bare outlines their complaint had a close resemblance to the grumbles of elderly gentlemen in any part of the world—the place was going to the dogs, it was the government's fault, the younger generation were irreligious, disobedient and depraved, over-taxation was ruining them, upstarts of low birth and odious manners were usurping the government offices, the police were corrupt, and so on. But there was this difference, that they were risking their lives to tell me these things and, behind their querulousness, I thought I could distinguish a genuine anxiety for the welfare of their people. Over-taxation was their main complaint; they belonged to a trading community and they saw its life being rapidly stifled by the impositions. They gave the facts in biblical detail—so many yards of cloth for the Governor, so many for the Emperor, so many houses commandeered by Abyssinian officials, so many days' forced labour by the women, so many by the men, such and such a percentage on each corn crop, so much on each basket of produce brought to market. It made a formidable list; a vast, increasing burden borne by everyone in the province, the advantage of which went directly and exclusively to the Abyssinian conquerors. There was no question of social services; the money went straight into the pockets of the officials. These were the arguments they put first as being of obvious practical importance, but later they began to talk in a more general way and I began to understand why they were prepared to risk their lives for the hope of reforms which, if ever possible, could only in the nature of things profit them for a very few years of life. They were concerned about a higher thing, the destruction of a culture. As boys they had known Harar as an independent Emirate; they had grown up in the Khoranic law, scholarship and habit of life. They saw their descendants not only reduced to political dependence—that they could have borne; indeed were clearly ready to bear it—but to cultural insignificance, losing both their religion and their racial identity, becoming not only under-dogs but mongrels. Moslem schools were being squeezed out; Moslem law was overruled by Abyssinian; drink was sold openly in the streets; the fasts were broken, ancient customs falling into decay; a Moslem who turned Christian was promoted, a Christian who turned Moslem was flogged; they spoke with horror of the contamination by Christian manners, in almost identical terms as those in which the Bishops' encyclicals denounce 'the New Paganism.'

I asked why, in this case, they wished to be governed by England, and they replied politely that they did not regard England as a really Christian people. We thought all religions of the same value; besides we were rich. The French were licentious

and poor, only one degree better than the Abyssinians.
They did not know much about the Italians but they
understood they were a good people. They frankly
hoped they would win the war. ' The Habasha '
(Abyssinians) ' order us to pray in the Mosque for
victory. Only Allah knows for whose victory we
pray.'

What they would most like to see would be a
bloodthirsty defeat of the Abyssinians by the Italians,
followed by a partition in which the Harar province
was added to British Somaliland. It was a states-
manlike aspiration, but I was not able to give them
much hope of its fulfilment.

No news of any value came from the front.
Wehib Pasha's defensive lines seemed to be holding
out. There was daily bombing in the Gorahai
and Sassa Baneh district. Everyone spoke of a big
offensive in the next few days. Desta's and
Nasebu's armies were now concentrated against
Graziani, who, it seemed, had received no reinforcements. We still believed that the big campaign
of the winter would be fought on the southern front.
At the beginning of November I returned to Addis
with the intention of collecting all my equipment
and taking up quarters in the consulate at Harar.

I arrived, however, to find that the long-awaited
permission to go to Dessye had at last been granted.
Enthusiasm for the trip had simultaneously begun to
wane. It was said that the Emperor would not in

fact go there; that it was a ruse to get the pressmen under close observation and out of harm's way; that there would be no wireless facilities; that the big southern campaign would begin in our absence. In the end only a small number of those who had been clamouring for permission decided to avail themselves of it. The Radical was among them, and he and I agreed to travel together.

As soon as this was known we became a centre of interest. All the boys at the Deutsches Haus, and the girl of no fixed occupation who pottered about the outbuildings giggling and occasionally appeared in the bedrooms with a broom, applied to accompany us. A saturnine Syrian, named Mr. Karam, who had lately formed the habit of waylaying me on Sunday mornings after Mass and asking me to drink coffee with him, offered to sell us a motor lorry. The trouble about this lorry was that it did not in fact belong to Mr. Karam. He had secured an option on it from a fellow Syrian and hoped to resell it at a profit. This was not clear until later, when he suffered great embarrassment about the spare parts. We said we would not take the lorry until it was fully equipped; he promised to equip it as soon as the agreement was signed. It was only when we went with him to the store that we discovered that he could not get the spare parts on credit, and could not pay for them until we had paid him an instalment of the price. There was a further embarrassment. We demanded a trial run up Entoto to test the engine. He could not get the petrol for the trip. In the end we filled up the tanks. James, who was not getting the rake-off he expected and had consequently taken up a suspicious attitude to Mr. Karam, reported in triumph next morning that Mr. Karam had hired out the lorry to a building contractor and was consuming our petrol. Poor Mr. Karam was merely trying to raise the money for a new tyre. In the end we hired the machine for a month, at what I suspect was very near its full purchase price. From that moment Mr. Karam was obsessed by anxiety that we proposed to make off with his lorry. He hung about the garage, where a gang was at work enhancing its value with a covered top and built-in boxes for petrol cans, pathetically canvassing our signatures to bits of paper on which we guaranteed not to drive beyond Dessye. It happened that the various agreements were made out in my name. When, a month later, the Radical and I separated and I returned to Addis Ababa in another car, poor Mr. Karam's suspicions became feverish. He was convinced that there had been a plot against him and that the Radical had deserted with his lorry to the Italians.

With James's help we got together a suitable staff for the journey. He and my own boy, an Abyssinian, had long been at enmity. In the hiring of the servants they frequently came to tears. The most important man was the cook. We secured one who looked, and as it turned out was, all that a cook should be. A fat, flabby Abyssinian with reproachful eyes. His chief claim to interest was that his former master, a German, had been murdered and dismembered in the Issa country. I asked him why he had done nothing to protect him. ' *Moi, je ne suis pas soldat, suis cuisinier vous savez.*' That seemed a praiseworthy attitude, so I engaged him. He suffered a great deal from the privations of the journey and cried with cold most evenings, the tears splashing and sizzling among the embers of his fire, but he cooked excellently, with all the native cook's aptitude for producing four or five courses from a single blackened pan over a handful of smoking twigs.

The chauffeur seemed to be suitable until we gave him a fortnight's wages in advance to buy a blanket. Instead he bought cartridges and *tedj*, shot up the bazaar quarter and was put in chains. So we engaged a Harari instead who formed a Moslem alliance with James against the other servants. The Radical and I found ourselves in almost continuous session as a court of arbitration. A cook's boy and chauffeur's boy completed the party. We had brought camping equipment and a fair quantity of stores from England; we supplemented these with flour, potatoes, sugar and rice from the local market; our Press cards were officially endorsed for the journey; our servants had been photographed and provided with special passes; and by November 13, the day announced by the Press Bureau for our departure, everything was ready.

ANTICLIMAX

It seemed scarcely possible that any working of the Addis bureaucracy could be so smooth. Eight or nine other parties were being fitted out for the journey, some on a very magnificent scale. One truck was emblazoned with the Lion of Judah and bore the legend ' —— *Co. Inc. of New York. EXPEDITION TO THE FRONT WITH H.M. THE EMPEROR OF ETHIOPIA.*' But few of us really believed that we should be allowed to start on the appointed day.

Rumours came back that there were disturbances on the Dessye road. Part of it ran through the fringe of the Danakil country and these unamiable people had been resorting to their traditional sport of murdering runners and stragglers from the Abyssinian forces; there had also been sharp fighting between the Imperial Guard and the irregular troops, causing a number of casualties which reached us in a highly exaggerated form. A Canadian journalist who had arranged to start a week earlier with a caravan of mules had his permission cancelled abruptly and without explanation. David and Lorenzo refused to commit themselves; both were unapproachable for the two days preceding the 13th, but on the night of the 12th no official announcement had been made of postponement, our passes were in order, and the Radical and I decided to see how far we could get. At the best we might arrive before the road had been cleared of traces of the recent troubles; at the worst it would be an interesting experiment with Ethiopian government methods. The correspondent of the *Morning Post* decided to join us.

Most of the loading was done on the day before. That night we kept the lorry in the road outside the Deutsches Haus and put two boys to sleep in it. We meant to start at dawn, but, just as we were ready, James accused the cook of peculation, the Abyssinians refused to be driven by a Harari, and my personal boy burst into tears. I think they had spent the evening saying goodbye to their friends and were suffering from hangovers. The only two who kept their composure were those who had guarded the lorry. It was nearly nine before everyone's honour was satisfied. The streets were then crowded and our lorry, painted with the names of our papers and flying the Union Jack, made a conspicuous object. We drove past the Press Bureau, glancing to see that there was no notice on the door. We let down the side curtains, and the three whites lay low among the cases of stores hoping that we should pass as a government transport.

Our chief fear was that we should find a barrier and military post at the city limits, of the kind which guarded the approach to Harar. For nearly an hour we sprawled under cover in extreme discomfort as the heavily laden lorry jolted and lurched along the rough track. Then James told us that all was clear. We sat up, tied back the curtains, and found we were in open country. Addis was out of sight; a few eucalyptus trees on the horizon behind us marked the extreme of urban expansion, before us lay a smooth grassy plain and the road, sometimes worn bare, scarred by ruts and hoof marks, sometimes discernible only by the boulders that had been distributed along it at intervals to trace its course. There was brilliant sunshine and a cool breeze. The boys at the back began to unwrap their bundles of luggage and consume large quantities of an aromatic spiced paste. An air of general good humour had succeeded the irritation of early morning.

We drove on for five or six hours without a stop. The way was easy; occasionally we met small streams where loose stones and sometimes a few baulks of timber had been piled to afford a crossing; for the most part we ran over firm, bare earth. This was still Galla country, for Menelik had founded his capital in conquered territory. We passed small farms, many of them stone built, standing beside hedges of euphorbia. Galla girls came out to wave to us, tossing their bundles of plaited hair. The men bowed low, three times; no one had travelled by car on that road for many months except Abyssinian officials or officers, and they had learned to associate motor traffic with authority.

After the first twenty miles we found soldiers everywhere. Some at noon, still encamped; others wandering along in companies of a dozen; some with mules to carry their loads, some with women. These were stragglers from Ras Getatchu's army which had gone through Addis a week before.

The road turned and wandered following the lie of the ground; every now and then we ran across the line of the telephone, a double overhead wire running straight across country. This, we knew, constituted our danger.

The first telephone station was named Koromach. We reached it at three o'clock. A uniformed Abyssinian stood across the road signalling us to stop. James and the Harari were all for running him down; we restrained their enthusiasm and climbed out of our places. The office was a small, lightless *tukal* a hundred yards or so off the road. There were twenty or thirty irregular soldiers there, squatting on their heels with rifles across their knees, and a chief in a new khaki uniform. By means of James the telephone officer explained that he had received an order from Addis to stop two car loads of white men travelling without permits. This constituted the strong point of our argument, for we were clearly only one car load and we had our permits; we showed them to him. He took them away into a corner and studied them at length; yes, he admitted, we had our permits. He showed them to the chief and the two sat for some time in colloquy. ' The chief is a good man,' said James. ' The telephone man very bad man. He is saying we are not to go on. The chief says we have permission and he will not stop us.'

Since the man in charge of the guns was on our side, we took a more arrogant line. What proof had the clerk that he had received a message at all? How did he know who was speaking? How did he know the message, if message there was, referred to us? Here were we being held up in our lawful business by the hearsay statement of the telephone. It was evident that the chief really distrusted the telephone as much as we affected to do. A piece of writing on a printed card had more weight with him than a noise coming out of a hole in the wall. At this stage of the discussion James left us and disappeared into the lorry. He returned a moment later with a bottle of whisky and a mug. We gave the chief a good half-pint of neat spirit. He tossed it off, blinked a little, and apologised for the delay we had been caused; then he conducted us, with his men, to the lorry and, the telephone man still protesting, waved us a cordial farewell.

We had been held up for half an hour. It got dark soon after six, so, since we had as yet had no practice in making camp, after an hour and a half's further drive, we turned off the track and stopped for the night under the lee of a small hill.

It was deadly cold. None of us slept much that night. I could hear the boys shivering and chattering round the fire whenever I woke. An hour before dawn we rose, breakfasted and struck camp under a blaze of stars. With the first sign of the sun we were on the road. Our hope was to get through Debra Birhan before the Gibbi officials at Addis were awake to warn them of our approach. Debra

Birhan was about three hours' drive away. It was the last telephone station on the road. Once past that the way lay clear to Dessye.

We were out of Galla country now and among true Abyssinians, but this part was sparsely populated and many of the farms had been left empty by their owners who were marching to the front. There were fields of maize here and there, standing high on either side of the road, many of them showing where they had been trampled down by passing soldiers; the track was tolerably level and we made good time. When we were a couple of miles from Debra Birhan, James warned us that it was time to hide. We drew the curtains, lay down as before and covered ourselves as well as we could with sacks and baggage.

It seemed a very long two miles and we had begun to believe that we were safely past the station when the lorry came to a halt and we heard a loud altercation going on all round us. We still lay low, hoping that James would bluff our way through, but after about five minutes his head appeared through the curtain. It was no good; rather shamefacedly we crept out of hiding. We found ourselves on the green of a large village. On one side stood the church of considerable size from which the place took its name. Next to it was the Governor's compound and courthouse; on all sides irregular clusters of huts; some sizeable trees; a pretty place. A less agreeable prospect was the collection of

soldiers who surrounded us. They were the crocks
left behind when the young men went to the war.
They were ragged and dilapidated, some armed with
spears but most of them with antiquated guns. 'I
am sorry to disturb you,' said James politely, 'but
these people wished to shoot us.'

In the centre stood the mayor—a typical Abyssinian squireen, tall, very fat, one-eyed. It was
not clear at first whether he was disposed to be
friendly; we tried him with whisky, but he said
he was fasting—a bad sign.

He said he had received a message to stop us.
We told him we had heard that story before at
Koromach; we had cleared the whole matter up
there. It was a mistake. We showed him our
permits. Yes, he admitted, they were quite in
order. He must just make a note of our names and
write a letter of commendation for us to the other
chiefs on the road; would we come with him to
Government House.

It sounded hopeful, but James added to his interpretation ' I think, sir, that this is a liar-man.'

A leper woman had now joined the party;
together we all sauntered across the green to the
mayor's compound.

The main building was a rectangular, murky hut.
We went inside. The telephone operator was not
well that day; he lay on his bed in the darkest
corner. The chief of police sat by his side: a
toothless little old man with an absurd military cap

on the side of his head. These three talked at some length about us. 'They do not want to let us go, but they are a little afraid,' said James. 'You must pretend to be angry.' We pretended to be angry. 'They are *very* afraid,' said James. But if this was so they controlled their emotion heroically.

The argument followed much the same course as yesterday's, but the one-eyed mayor was much less impressed by our written permits. First he affected not to be able to read them; then he complained that the signature looked fishy; then he said that although we had indeed permission to go to Dessye we had neglected to get permission to leave Addis Ababa. It was a mere formality, he said; we had better go back and do it.

Then we made a false step. We proposed that he should do this for us by telephone. He jumped at the suggestion. It was exactly what he would do. Only it would take some time. It was unsuitable that people of our eminence should stand about in the sun. Why did we not pitch a tent and rest? His men would help us.

If we had gone on being angry we might still have got through; instead we weakly assented, pitched a tent and sat down to smoke. After an hour I sent James to inquire how things were getting on. He came back to say that no attempt was being made to telephone to Addis. We must come back and be angry again.

We found the chief holding a court, his single,

beady eye fixed upon a group of litigants who at a
few inches' distance from him were pleading their
case with all the frantic energy common in Abyssinian
suits.   He was not at all pleased at being disturbed.
He was a great man, he said.   We said we were
great men too.   He said that the telephone operator
was far from well, that the line was engaged, that
the Gibbi was empty, that it was a fast day, that it
was dinner-time, that it was late, that it was early,
that he was in the middle of important public
business, that James was offensive and untruthful
and was not translating what he said and what we
said, but instead, was trying to make a quarrel of a
simple matter which admitted of only one solution,
that we should wait until the afternoon and then
come and see him again.

I do not know what James said, but the result was
an adjournment of the court and a visit to the telephone hut, where the chief of police demonstrated,
by twirling the handle, that the machine was out of
order.   We wrote out a telegram to Lorenzo protesting in the customary terms of the Foreign Press
Association that we were being unjustly held prisoner
in defiance of his own explicit permission to proceed.   We had little hope of moving Lorenzo;   we
thought it might impress the mayor.   'They are
very frightened,' said James.   But they proceeded to
their luncheon with the utmost composure and our
message remained in the hands of the bedridden and
now, apparently, moribund telephonist.   'They

are too frightened to send it,' said James, trying to put an honourable complexion on the affair.

When we returned to our tent we found that, in our absence, the entire male and female labour of the village had been recruited and a barricade built of stones and tree trunks across the front of the lorry. Walking a little way back along the road we had come, we found another barricade. Any hopes which we might have entertained of the mayor's goodwill were now dispelled.

The afternoon passed in a series of fruitless negotiations. The chief would not send our message to Lorenzo, nor subsequent messages which we wrote to other officials. We tried to get him to endorse them with a note that they had been presented and refused. That was no good. We made up our minds to spending the night at Debra Birhan and pitched the other tents.

Our sudden docility disconcerted the chief and for the first time he showed some sign of the fears which James had attributed to him. He clearly feared that we intended to make a sortie by night. To prevent this he tried to separate us from the lorry; he and the chief of police came waddling down at the head of their guard—now reinforced by the village idiot, a stark-naked fellow who loped and gibbered among them until they drove him away with stones, when he squatted out of range and spent the rest of the day gesticulating at them obscenely. They said that we had chosen a very cold and dangerous camping ground. We might be attacked by robbers or lions; the tents might be blown down; would we not prefer to move to a more sheltered place? We replied that if they had been solicitous of our comfort earlier, we could no doubt have found a better camping ground on the road to Dessye.

Later they tried a stupendous lie. The Emperor was on the telephone, they said; he had rung up to say that ten lorry loads of journalists were on the way to join us; would we mind waiting for them until to-morrow morning, when we could all travel together ?

Finally, to make things certain, they set a guard round us; not a mere posse of sentries but the whole village, leper, idiot, police chief and the mayor himself. The latter pitched a tent a few paces from us; a ramshackle square thing which to the loud derision of our boys, who were enjoying the situation to the full, blew down twice. The others squatted with spears and rifles in a circle all round us. It was a bitterly cold night. By dawn they looked frozen. We breakfasted, struck camp, loaded the lorry and waited. At eight the chief came to say that we must go back. The barrier behind us was removed. We climbed into the lorry. Even now the chief feared a sudden dash for Dessye; he drew up his men across the road with their rifles ready. The chief of police spoiled the gravity of the defence by trotting forward and asking us to take his photograph. Then, in a cheerful mood, we drove back to Addis Ababa, which with some rather ruthless driving we made before nightfall.

Our little trip had caused a mild scandal. As soon as it became known we had gone, officials from the Press Bureau had trotted round all the hotels with typewritten notices, dated the day before, saying that leave for Dessye was indefinitely postponed. A stout barricade and a military post were set up on the road out of Addis. The French journalists had lodged a formal protest that preferential treatment was being given us; Belattingetta Herui announced that we were enjoying a little holiday in camp five miles outside the capital; an American journalist cabled home that we were in chains. Mr. Karam hung round us rather tentatively offering a bill for ten pounds; the return trip to Debra Birhan, he claimed, had not been specified in our original contract. We had missed no news of importance and had picked up through James, who had earned the esteem of one of our guards with the present of six matches, some interesting details of the Danakil raids and inter-regimental fighting near Dessye. On the whole it had been an enjoyable excursion.

5

Two days after our return general permission for Dessye was again issued, this time in earnest. Rumours, which proved groundless, of an Italian advance in the Fafan valley, drew a scamper of journalists to Harar, among them the correspondents of *The Times*, the *Morning Post*, and Reuter's. Patrick was still happily cruising round the Red Sea. In the end it was a scratch caravan which set out for Dessye. The Radical, the *Daily Express* correspondent and I were the only regular English journalists; an American preacher, a free-lance communist, and an unemployed German Jew deputised for more august principals. Only the cinema companies travelled impressively.

We started on the 19th and travelled without incident. We went in our own time. There was no possible advantage to be gained by priority, but habitual competition had by now unbalanced many, so that some lorries made a race of it, and neglected the common decencies of travel, passing by without offer of help a rival outfit stuck in a river bed. An adolescent Canadian far outdistanced the rest of the field and arrived in Dessye a day ahead; I believe that on his return he was accorded a civic reception in his home town for this feat. Others preferred a more leisurely journey; stopped to fish and shoot on the way and compose descriptions of the scenery, which, a few hours after Debra Birhan, became varied and magnificent.

It was intensely cold on the plateau, with a continuous high wind. Sometimes we passed a handful of stragglers from one of the migrating armies; sometimes a slave or a free cultivator working in the fields, but it was mostly desolate country, bounded by a horizon of ever-receding ranges of blue mountain; occasionally the hills to our right fell away and revealed a sensational prospect of the Awash valley and Danakil plain, shimmering in the heat thousands of feet below.

Early in the afternoon of the second day we came suddenly and without warning—for the road was recent and not yet marked on any published map—upon an enormous escarpment, a rocky precipice open before our wheels; far below lay a broad valley, richly cultivated and studded with small hemi-spherical hills, each crowned with a church or a cluster of huts. Down this awful cliff the track fell in a multitude of hairpin bends; surveyed from above the gradient seemed, in places, almost per-pendicular; there was barely clearance for the wheels; on the off-side the edge crumbled away into space; at the corners the road was sharply inclined in the wrong direction. Our Harari driver gave a sigh of despair. Straight down the face of the cliff transecting the road at each turn led a precipitous footpath. Nominally to lighten the truck, actually because we were thoroughly scared, the Radical and I decided to go down on foot. It was a stiff descent; with every step the air became warmer as though we were scrambling across the seasons. When we reached more tolerable ground we waited for the lorry, which presently arrived, the driver speechless but triumphant All that night, James reported, he was talking in his sleep about braking and reversing.

We found a warm and sheltered camping place a few miles from the foot of the escarpment, and here, shortly before sundown, we were visited by heralds from the local governor, Dedjasmach Matafara, who was living near by in temporary quarters, to ask us our business. I sent James to explain. He returned rather drunk to say that the Dedjasmach was ' very gentleman.' He was accompanied by slaves bearing a present of *tedj*, native bread and a young sheep; also an invitation to breakfast the next morning.

The Dedjasmach was a very old man, a veteran of the first battle of Adowa, corpulent, ponderous in his movements, with unusually dark skin and a fine white beard. He bore a marked resemblance to the portraits of the Emperor Menelik. His normal residence was some way off at Ankober; he was here on duty patrolling the road.

He occupied a series of huts behind a well-made stockade. There was a circular *tukal* where he slept and where, on our arrival, he was completing his toilet; there was a larger, square building for eating and the transaction of business, a cook-house, women's and soldiers' quarters, and in the centre an open space, part farmyard and part barrack square. Soldiers, slaves and priests thronged the place, disputing it with cattle and poultry.

James stood at our side to interpret. The Dedjasmach greeted us with great politeness and dignity, slipped on a pair of elastic-sided boots and led us across to the dining-room. The preparations were simple. One of the sheets was taken from the Dedjasmach's bed and stretched across the centre of the hut to shield us from public view; behind it, in almost complete darkness, a low wicker table was laid with piles of native bread. The Radical and I, the Dedjasmach and two priests, sat down at little stools. James stood beside us. Two women slaves stood with horsehair whisks, fanning away the flies. Abyssinian bread is made in thin, spongy discs. It is used very conveniently as both plate and spoon. The curry—a fiery but rather delicious dish which forms the staple food of those who can afford it— is ladled out into the centre of the bread; morsels are then wrapped up in pieces torn from the edge and put into the mouth. The Dedjasmach courteously helped us to tit-bits from his own pile. Other slaves brought us horn mugs of *tedj*—a heavy drink at eight in the morning. Conversation was intermittent and rather laborious; it consisted chiefly of questions addressed to us by our host and the priests. They asked us our ages, whether we were married, how many children. One of the priests recorded this information in a little exercise book. The Dedjas-mach said he loved the English because he knew that they too hated the Italians. The Italians were a poor sort of people, he said; one of his friends had killed forty of them, one after the other, with his sword. He asked us if we knew General Harrington;

he had been a good man; was he still alive? Then he returned to the question of the Italians. They did not like the smell of blood, he said; when they smelled blood they were afraid; when an Abyssinian smelled blood he became doubly brave; that was why the sword was better than the gun.

Besides, he said, the Italians disliked fighting so much they had to be given food free before they would do it; he knew this for a fact; he had seen it himself forty years ago; they had great carts loaded with food and wine to persuade the men to fight; Abyssinians scorned that; each man brought his own rations and, if he had one, his own mule. He asked us when the Emperor was going to the war; that was where he should be, with his soldiers. The Abyssinians fought better if the Emperor were looking on; each strove to attract his attention with deeds of valour.

Water was brought for us to bathe our hands; then little cups of bitter coffee. Finally we made our adieux. He invited us, when the troubles were over, to come and visit him at Ankober. He asked us to take two soldiers with us to Dessye; we pointed out that our lorry was already overladen, but he insisted, saying that some people had been killed on the road lately. Slightly drunk, we stepped out into the brilliant morning sunshine. One of the soldiers who was accompanying us had to sell his mule before he could start. At last the transaction was complete. He bundled in at the back with the boys; we were saved the embarrassment of the second by the arrival, just as we were starting, of a French journalist. We told him that the Dedjasmach had sent the soldier for him and he accepted the man gratefully.

Then we resumed the journey.

It had been more than a pleasant interlude; it had been a glimpse of the age-old, traditional order that still survived, gracious and sturdy, out of sight beyond the brass bands and bunting, the topees and humane humbug of Tafari's régime; of an order doomed to destruction. Whatever the outcome of the present war: mandate or conquest or internationally promoted native reform — whatever resulted at Geneva or Rome or Addis Ababa, Dedjasmach Matafara and all he stood for was bound to disappear. But we were pleased to have seen it and touched hands across the centuries with the court of Prester John.

On the fourth day we reached Dessye. The second part of the journey was varied and enjoyable. We crossed several streams and one considerable river where we stuck for several hours, unloaded and finally heaved the truck clear on our shoulders, but there were no serious obstacles to compare with the escarpment; we passed a hot spring and an army —Dedjasmach Bayana's, which had left Addis fourteen days before; they had found a sugar plantation, and every man was sucking a cane as he shambled along; Bayana himself maintained the same pomp as when he had paraded before the Emperor; he rode under a black umbrella, surrounded by his domestic slaves and led-mules still adorned with their ceremonial trappings; a team of women followed him carrying jars of *tedj* under crimson cotton veils. We passed through belts of forest, full of birds and game and monkeys and brilliant flowers. Then the road suddenly improved in quality and began to mount. It took an hour to reach the town from the moment when we came into sight. It lay high up in a cup in the mountains, surrounded on all sides by hills; the road from Addis twisted and doubled, led through a narrow pass into the city, and out again to the north, where it led direct to the front for twenty miles and then petered out into the original caravan track.

Dessye is a place of recent creation; an Abyssinian military outpost in the Mohammedan Wollo country. In appearance it was very much like a miniature of Addis Ababa—the same eucalyptus trees, the same single shopping street, the same tin roofs, a Gibbi built on an eminence dominating the town. There were a few Armenian storekeepers, an American Adventist Mission at the extremity of the town, a French Mission a mile or so distant. The most solid building was the former Italian consulate, deserted now, and, it was rumoured, under preparation for the Emperor's coming. The inhabitants were Abyssinian squatters; the Wollo Gallas came in for the weekly market but lived in the villages. There was a large Coptic Church and a building, ecclesiastical in appearance, which was in reality the private house of the Dedjasmach. At the time of our arrival this building was flying the Red Cross in honour of the two Irishmen who had lately arrived, and an anti-aircraft gun was mounted on the balcony.

The place was full of soldiers; a detachment of the Imperial Guard was quartered in the grounds of the Italian consulate; the irregulars slept in a ring of encampments along the surrounding hillside. They came into town at dawn and remained until sunset, drinking, quarrelling and sauntering about the streets; more were arriving daily and the congestion was becoming perilous. The chiefs were under orders to leave for the front, but they hung on, saying that they would not move until the Emperor led them in person. It was partly for this purpose that his arrival was expected.

We reported to the mayor, a stocky, bearded figure who had disgraced himself in London and now happily compromised in his costume between the new and old régimes by wearing beard and cloak of a traditional cut and, below them, shorts and red and white ringed football stockings. He passed us on to the chief of police, who, that afternoon, was tipsy. Eventually we found a camping ground for ourselves in the compound of the local branch of the Ethiopian Bank, an institution of indiscernible value, for it could neither cash cheques, change notes or accept deposits. Here we spent the first night, moving next day to the Adventist Mission, who hospitably threw open their large park to the journalists.

For so many weeks now Dessye had been our goal—a promised land sometimes glimpsed from afar, sometimes impenetrably obscured, sometimes seen in a mirage a stone's throw away in crystal detail, always elusive, provocative, desirable—that its pursuit had become an end in itself. Now that, at length, we found ourselves actually there, when the tents were pitched and the stores unpacked and all round us a village of tents had sprung up, we began to wonder what precisely we had gained by the journey. We were two hundred or so miles nearer the Italians, but for any contact we had with the battle-field or information about what was happening, we were worse off than at Addis Ababa. A field wireless had been established on the hillside a mile out of the town. Here we all hurried to enquire about facilities and were told, to our surprise, that messages of any length might be sent. At Addis there had been a limit of two hundred words. All messages from Dessye had to be retransmitted from Addis. It seemed odd, but we were used to unaccountable happenings. That evening all over the camp typewriters were tapping as the journalists spread themselves over five hundred, eight hundred, a thousand words messages describing the perils of the journey. Two days later we were cheerfully informed that none of the messages had been sent, that no more could be accepted until further notice, that when the station reopened there would be a limit of fifty words and a rigid censorship. So there, for the time being, our professional activities ended.

A week passed in complete idleness. The Emperor's arrival was daily predicted and daily postponed. Lij Yasu died, and James, who had been dining with Mohammedan friends in the town, and drinking in Christian fashion, returned in a high state of excitement to say that the Emperor would be murdered if he attempted to show himself among the Wollo Gallas.

An Abyssinian gentleman named Dedjasmach Gugsa Ali enjoyed what must be one of the briefest periods of official favour in recorded history; he was the former governor of a neighbouring district, had been deposed, and had lived for many years in disgrace. He now followed the prevailing fashion and presented himself at the Gibbi and offered his submission. The governing Dedjasmach reinstated him, and in the name of the Emperor embraced him. Bowing low, Gugsa Ali withdrew from his presence, tripped over the doorstep and broke his neck.

The native members of the ' Ethiopian Red Cross ' had a beano, stripped to the skin and danced round the tent of their American officer, who had only that evening moved his quarters to avoid contamination from his more worldly Irish colleagues.

ANTICLIMAX

The governing Dedjasmach made a strenuous and partly successful attempt to get some of the soldiers to the front. He organised a parade, and himself at their head, drums beating and bugles playing, led them Pied-Piper fashion up the Makale road, returning by himself after dark to the more agreeable accommodation of his own bedroom.

Every item of news became known to us all simultaneously; there was no hope of a scoop; the wireless station remained blandly obstructive. Relieved of the itch to cable the journalists displayed amiable characteristics which they had hitherto concealed. We became house proud; the Radical and I set a popular vogue by erecting the first latrine. Mr. Prospero contrived an arc-light. We began to entertain and competed mildly in kitchen and service. Except for a Finnish misanthrope who maintained a front of unbroken hostility—and later on his return to Addis indulged in litigation at the American consular court against a colleague who punched him— the grimmest characters seemed to grow soft in idleness. On November 28 there was a Thanksgiving Dinner, attended by all except the Finn, and after it a drinking competition won—dishonestly we discovered later—by one of the Irishmen.

Next day it was announced officially that the Emperor was on the road, and on the 30th he arrived. The soldiers waited for him all day, squatting along the route, reeling and jostling about the streets. They had been surly and hostile for some days; now, exhilarated at the prospect of the Emperor's arrival, they became menacing, held up the cars of the cinema men, scowled and jeered through the heat of the day; then, towards evening, as it became cold, crowded shivering and morose. The royal mules in brilliant saddle cloths waited to take the Emperor on the last stage of his journey, up the hill to the Crown Prince's Gebbi, but the sun went down, the crowds began to melt away and the photographers were again deprived of a picturesque shot. At length he arrived, unobtrusively, in the darkness. From now on Dessye became his headquarters; in the new year he moved north; he was not to see Addis again until he arrived in the spring, in flight to the coast.

With the Emperor came a small circle of courtiers, including Lorenzo and David, and with them the official news. We had left Addis in the expectation of a big Italian attack in the Fafan; it was now announced that the attack had completely failed, that Ras Desta had gained a decisive victory and that bands of Ethiopian Somalis were invading Italian territory and carrying out successful raids as far as the coast. In the north the Italian advance had come to an end; the garrison at Makale was almost cut off and a great concentration of troops at Amba Alagi—Imru's, Kassa's and Moulugetta's—were preparing to surround it. There was no mistaking the sincerity of the Court's optimism; three weeks before they had professed the same confidence but in a strained and anxious fashion; now, away from the tin and tarmac of Addis, in the keen air of the mountains, reverting to the simpler habits of their upbringing, they were openly jubilant.

Next day the Emperor came to visit the American hospital. The wards were fairly full, but not with war wounded; there were several venereal cases and some of influenza contracted on the journey up (the Imperial Guard seemed to be of lower stamina than the irregular troops); there were a few soldiers who had deserted from Eritrea and got badly cut up by a company of Abyssinian troops deserting in the opposite direction; but there were no heroes upon whom the Emperor could suitably manifest his sympathy. In order to show the equipment of the hospital at its best advantage the doctors staged an operation—the amputation of a gangrened stump of arm. Emperor, Court and journalists crowded into the theatre; the photographers and cinema men took their shots. The Emperor asked, ' And where did this gallant man lose his hand? '

' Here in Dessye. The Dedjasmach had it cut off for stealing two besas worth of corn.'

Meanwhile in Europe and America the editors and film magnates had begun to lose patience. They had spent large sums of money on the Abyssinian war and were getting very little in return; several journalists had already been recalled; the largest cinema company was beginning to pack up; now a general retreat began. I received my dismissal by cable on the day after the Emperor's arrival. For a few hours I considered staying on independently. That had been my original intention, but now the prospect seemed unendurably dismal. I had long wanted to spend Christmas at Bethlehem. This was the opportunity.

The war seemed likely to drag on without incident until the big rains; peace terms disappointing to both sides and heavy with future dangers would be devised and accepted. There would be an exchange of territory; Italy, after its ceremonious occupation, would clearly keep Adowa, perhaps the whole of the Tigre; Abyssinia would get an outlet to the sea, either at Assab or Zeila. Neither port would be valuable without European or American exploitation. The old wrangle, now acutely embittered, of competing concession hunters, spheres of influence, zenophobic local officials, obstructionist central government—the very situation which had brought about the present war—would begin anew. Disorder in the provinces, immensely aggravated by the recent profuse distribution of arms and munitions, would again challenge intervention. Perhaps there would be an attempt to put into effect the suggestions of the Five Power Conference in September; there might be an administration by international foreign advisers; their work, difficult enough among a people slightly scared at the unknown dangers of mechanised invasion, would be utterly impossible after a successful defence; the natural truculence of the Shoans would be confirmed by an absolute conviction of their superiority and invincibility. Italy would certainly be unrepresented in the foreign régime and her imperialist aspirations unsatisfied. There would be a complete end of any peaceful penetration; there would be a development loan and international bond holders would call for intervention. If it was to be effective, the international régime would find itself transformed into a coercive protectorate; perhaps a mandate would be granted to England and France—or at the worst to both; there might be an expensive war of conquest under League auspices; the sanctionist movement would appear to the whole world—as it already appeared to part of it—as a device of the great imperial powers to cut out a competitor.

There were still plenty of munitions and plenty of men in Abyssinia; there was on all sides an apparent zeal for the Emperor's cause. We knew that there was disaffection and disorganisation, but no one realised how fragile had been the whole structure of order in the country. Neither then in December, nor in the subsequent two months, did anyone in Abyssinia or Rome seriously anticipate the sudden, utter collapse of the Shoa monarchy.

Wherever one's sympathies lay—it was a situation in which an Englishman could have little enthusiasm either way—there seemed grounds for nothing except despond and exasperation. In this mood I left Dessye. There was a car travelling to Addis Ababa on Red Cross business in which I was able, illegally, to purchase a seat. We had to start before dawn in order to avoid notice from the Red Cross authorities. I took one servant, rations for the road, and left everything else with the Radical. James cried. It was an uneventful journey. The German driver—an adventurous young airman who had come to look for good fortune after serving in the Paraguayan war—kept a rifle across the wheel and inflicted slight wounds on the passing farmers at point-blank range.

Addis was dead. With the Emperor's departure the public services had settled into the accustomed coma. The bars were open but empty. A handful of journalists from the south were packing up to return to England. The mystery men had faded away.

After a few days I got down to Djibouti. At Diredawa the French garrison were firmly entrenched; half the town was a French fort. Djibouti was still crowded, still panicky. There were a number of journalists there reporting the war at leisure from their imaginations. One of them waged a pretty little war in his hotel bedroom with flags and a large scale map; others were still happily photographing scenes of Abyssinian home life in the *quartier toleré*. Soon after I left some bombs had been dropped on Dessye and the chief excitement of Djibouti centred on a race to get the films of them back to Europe.

ANTICLIMAX

Weeks later in Devon I saw them on the news reel. It was difficult to recapture the excitement, secrecy and competition that had attended their despatch.

News of the Hoare-Laval proposals reached us in the Red Sea; at Port Said we heard of their reception. Next day I was in Jerusalem and visited the Abyssinian monks, perched in their little African village on the roof of the Holy Sepulchre; Christmas morning in Bethlehem; desert and ruined castles in Transjordan; like the rest of the world I began to forget about Abyssinia.

VI

ADDIS ABABA DURING THE FIRST DAYS OF THE ITALIAN EMPIRE

I

BUT it was not so easy. With the withdrawal of the special correspondents, news from Abyssinia became meagre and inconspicuous ; soon it consisted mainly of the official communiqués issued by the rival governments. In February, Desta's army was routed on the Southern front and Graziani pursued him to Negelli. But this was not the advance we had expected. The Jijiga front was unbroken ; strategists still saw the campaign in terms of the Fafan route and the railway ; it was not yet realised that Badoglio would attempt and perform the stupendous feat of taking Addis Ababa from the North. In March, for the first time, English editors began to give preference to the Italian bulletins. In April it was clear that the Abyssinian armies were in a bad way, but the Emperor's flight in the beginning of May surprised the world. Some vivid accounts followed of anarchy and destruction. Then on the arrival of the Italians the last foreign journalists left the country and the English newspapers stopped printing Abyssinian news. There were other crises, the German occupation of the Rhine frontier, the Spanish civil war.

Sanctions were abolished after a few hours' debate. The Liberals, who in the preceding months had emerged from the shadows, so swollen with indignation as to become a bogey to their peaceable fellow citizens, were allowed to deflate, noisily but without much harm, in the correspondence columns of the Conservative press. Some memorable phrases were devised ; one indignant letter writer described the areas given over to banditry, where the Italians had not yet established garrisons, as ' pockets of legitimate government.'

It is by no means the first time in English history that the world has been almost fatally confused by mistaking the peevish whinny of the nonconformist conscience for the voice of the nation. It often happens. Someone is always the loser for it. This time it was the unfortunate Emperor of Abyssinia. The country—except for its perennial distrust of the Mediterranean races—was apathetic.

But for those of us who knew Abyssinia it was not so easy. There were countless loose ends. Why had Abyssinia broken up so suddenly ? How was the new régime really working ? Where were the Italian garrisons ? Had the Government of the West any real existence ? Were the submissions of the Rases genuine ? What had happened to David and James and M. Idot ? I received weekly copies of a paper devoted to Abyssinian propaganda, edited by an English suffragette ; it was full of startling stories of the state of the country. The continental papers printed an interview with Ras Seyoum in which he was reported as saying, ' I think your aeroplanes are marvellous.' The missionary who had described in harrowing terms the sufferings of a nation whose women and children were being blinded by gas, now wrote to say that their sight had been restored. What was really happening ? Curiosity could only be satisfied by another visit. Accordingly, at the beginning of June, I applied for permission to return. At the end of July it was granted.

I was the first Englishman to get into the country since its occupation and it seemed reasonable to expect that I should be able to sell a few articles to the newspapers. A year before every scrap of information and conjecture had been avidly gobbled up. But now the subject was dead except for the dribble of complaint in the correspondence column. The attitude of Fleet Street was typified when, one morning shortly before my departure, I received a letter from an editor saying, in terms which had then grown familiar, that he regretted that there was no longer any interest in Abyssinian conditions ; beside it on the breakfast-tray lay that morning's issue of his paper and prominently displayed on its middle page a letter written from an address in England by an Englishman who, I think, had no possible access to special information, describing the distress prevalent in Abyssinia, and calling upon Italy to redeem her ' tarnished honour ' by relieving it.

So, independent of any commissions from Fleet Street, drawn by motives of curiosity which seemed, in the stifling passage of the Red Sea, daily less compelling, I found myself once more in Djibouti, where eight months before I had taken ship with the fervent resolve never, in any circumstances, to set foot there again.

The place was uninhabitable. The hotels were full ; rows of Italian officers lying restlessly in camp beds and on tables in the public rooms gave them at night the appearance of improvised hospitals. The shifting population of polyglot refugees was now swollen by recent extraditions from up the line. Sitting in Regas's café one was able to count the familiar figures lounging past, with their familiar, questing faces. I had not been there ten minutes before I was joined by a Greek informer. ' The Italians will not let you go to Addis Ababa. They have even expulsed me.'

I told him that I already had my visa. He shook his head sagely.

' Mr. Waugh, do not go there. You have no idea what the conditions are up country. The

Italians are starving. The soldiers live on a piece of bread a day. Nothing can be bought in the shops. No one will accept the Italian money. The Abyssinians are encamped all round the town. Dessye has been evacuated. The Italians hold Addis Ababa, the railway line and the road to Makale—beyond that nothing. Last week they were still attempting to take Ankober. No one can go a hundred yards outside the town. Last month the railway was cut for ten days. Bandits march into the town whenever they like. They are fighting every day in the centre of the town. All the natives have arms hidden. When the Italians made an order for them to be given up they brought in only the old rifles. Every tukal has a new machine gun under the floor. Only last month they captured a train of lorries on the Dessye road and took all the ammunition. At a given signal the people will rise and massacre the Italians. By the twenty-fifth of September Addis will be in the hands of the Abyssinians. This time they will spare no one. Even the Gallas have turned against the Italians. They were given all kinds of promises and nothing has been done. They say in Europe that the war is over. It is only beginning. The people have got rid of Tafari. Now they can fight in their own way.'

It was the old Djibouti story adapted to the new conditions. One had heard it before in another form. It was never credible but it never failed to depress. For half an hour he poured out his warnings. Then he took his leave. ' I hope to come to England soon. Mr. Balfour will be *very* pleased to see me. I will visit you too in your home.'

The Somali hawkers loped in and out among the crowd selling cheroots, shirts and native daggers. Among them were two or three who had seen European service in the preceding year.

' Good evening, sir. I brought you a letter once from Mr. Collins when you were staying at the Consulate at Harar.' . . . ' Good evening, Mr. Waugh, did you find the hat you lost at Diredawa ? ' . . . ' How is Mr. Balfour ? ' . . . ' Do you remember me, sir ? I was with Mr. Roper. My brother-in-law was shot with the British major.' . . . ' How is the American with red hair ? ' . . . ' Good evening, sir, it was I who drove Captain P.'s motor when you had dinner with him at Addis Ababa.'

Their memory and curiosity were amazing. Once they were recognised they forgot about their merchandise and asked searching questions about the subsequent histories of the journalists. Were they married ; when were they coming back to Ethiopia. I asked some of them how they liked the new régime. There was plenty of work, they said ; some Somalis were making good money. I tried to press the point ; did the Somalis like being ruled by the Italians. Some Somalis made plenty of money, they said, others not so much.

' But are you glad the Emperor went away ? '

' Those that make money are glad. Some are sorry.'

' Why are they sorry ? '

' Because they do not make money.'

The train next day was densely crowded, almost exclusively by Italians—soldiers, government officials, traders, engineers, prospectors. It was impossible at this stage to distinguish them, for they were obliged to travel through French territory in civilian clothes. There was a general in plus-fours. An artillery officer who had been on my ship and who, through the heat of the Red Sea, had paraded the decks in riding boots and spurs, now appeared in crumpled shorts. It was a curious spectacle to see the rear-guard of a conquering army queueing up, presenting their passports, buying their railway tickets in an unfamiliar foreign currency, struggling with porters over their suitcases, as they made their entry into the new empire. Some, who had not got their mufti unpacked, had to unpick the stars and decorations from their tunics with nail scissors. It was a temporary inconvenience. During my stay in Abyssinia the agreement was made with France about the control of the railway ; meanwhile the French officials insisted rigidly on every formality, with, as I found later at Diredawa, a substantial profit to someone over the currency regulations.

There was a perceptible thrill of enthusiasm throughout the train as we crossed into Italian territory. The section of the line between the frontier and Diredawa was fairly secure and the guards were not much larger than they had been under the old régime, but there were patriotic demonstrations at each station, often broken by cordial shouts of recognition as a soldier ran up to the running-board to greet a friend.

Diredawa, like every place I visited in the country, was enormously full. The French garrison—about six hundred strong—was still there. In addition there was a large Italian camp and air base. Here, too, travellers were sleeping three or four to a room. The streets in the evening were thronged with soldiers, sauntering about in groups, looking like schoolboys on a wet Sunday of term, as soldiers always do look who have few duties and very little pocket-money.

It seemed suitable to begin my tour with a visit to the devastated areas. Accordingly next day I drove over to Harar and spent two nights with my former host at the British Consulate. He is a man who shuns publicity and for that reason alone I have been obliged to omit any detailed description of his achievements during the preceding eighteen months. From the attack on Walwal until the time of his departure, shortly after my visit, he worked alone in circumstances of constant anxiety, aggravated at the end by a grave attack of fever. He dealt with a situation of the utmost delicacy and responsibility, a responsibility out of all proportion to his seniority in his service. It is too little to say—but it is all I dare say without fear of antagonising him and betraying his hospitality—that of the honours distributed among the various Englishmen who distinguished themselves in Abyssinia during this unhappy period, none was more admirably earned than his.

I spent a day walking about the city, calling on people I had known before, visiting the bazaars and public buildings, wandering about in the lanes, peering into the *tedj* houses. A few months before it had been bombarded, burned, and—it was reported in the English press—sacked. Patrick Balfour had written an eloquent lament for it, headed ' *This was a City.*' It was practically unchanged. It was a little cleaner. The paving of the main streets was rather smoother. There were a great number of Italians about and fewer Abyssinians. The third best café was now called the Albergo Savoia. Most of the shops displayed pictures of Mussolini and the King of Italy. But in its general aspect it was the same city. The Hararis had come back in crowds ; their gay costume filled the streets. The market, which had been almost squeezed out of existence by Abyssinian impositions, was now going merrily. Merrily was the word. There could be no two opinions about whether the Hararis liked the change. They could now bring their produce into the town free of duty ; the labour which had before been conscripted was now voluntary and, by local standards, highly paid. The Indians looked sulky. The currency restrictions hit them hard. They were now obliged to spend their money in the country where they earned it and that is not the way of the East African Indian trader. The Abyssinian priests, depleted in number by the religious enthusiasm of the Somali bands, looked less than comfortable. But the Hararis were clearly in the best of humours.

People write and speak as though in the first few hours of the next war all the capital cities of Europe will be turned to dust. The Italian aeroplanes had had the place to themselves without any opposing aircraft or any serious interference from the ground, but the ravages of the bombardment were hard to find. There had always been a large proportion of ruinous houses in Harar. They were still there, many black from the recent fire. The rest had been repaired, almost effortlessly. The town was nearly empty at the time of the attack. When the inhabitants returned they had shovelled out the débris, patched the roofs, and settled down to their normal life. The buildings which had taken it worst were the Abyssinian church, the drawing-room of the French doctor, and the Catholic church. There government workmen were still engaged in restoration. It was a revelation to me to see how little damage a bomb does. The Catholic church had suffered a direct hit from a standard bomb. The roof was new but there were the same pictures on the walls, the same plaster statues, the same carved woodwork. There were a number of splinter holes, but one had to go round with a guide and have the damage pointed out. Throughout the entire campaign the heaviest casualties from air raids seem always to have been caused not by bombs, but by machine-gunning from the air.

The day was brilliant ; the night limpid cool. The consulate garden was full of highly coloured birds. There was no shortage of food ; the market was full of fruit, green vegetables and the best possible coffee. The consulate cow was in milk. Even the news that a party of bandits, eight hundred rifles strong, had been sauntering across the Diredawa road a week before, could not destroy the feeling of secure well-being. By contrast Addis was a place of sepulchral gloom.

The approach was miserable. The Somali-Abyssinian borders have always been a paradise for the money changer. At the moment they presented a microcosm of the world monetary chaos. There were seven sorts of currency of fluctuating value. First the lira which had been proclaimed the official money of the country ; but notes of 500 or 1000 lire carried the disadvantage that, though they were current at par within the territory, it was criminal to cross the frontier either way in their possession ; they were liable to confiscation at the customs and thus could only be changed for notes of lower denomination at a 20 per cent. discount. There were, as always, the two sorts of franc, Banque de France and Banque d'Indo-Chine, which have long proved a source of petty exaction at Djibouti. These might be exported and imported freely and were thus greatly in demand ; one could change them into lire very profitably but illegally. Then there was the Maria Theresa thaler which was still nominally current. This had been fixed at the value of 5 lire, with the result that it had instantly disappeared from circulation. It was still the only coin acceptable to natives outside Addis and Dire-dawa. Then there were the notes of the Bank of Ethiopia which no one used to want but which had now attained a sudden and temporary vogue, in spite of the liquidation of the Bank, because they were the official currency of the French railway ; and finally there were the nickel half- and quarter-thalers which, though they were still legal tender, no one wanted at any price.

The complexity of the situation was impressed on me when I attempted to buy my railway ticket from Diredawa to Addis. I came to the guichet with a wallet full of lire and francs. The clerk informed me I must pay in thalers. Where was I to get them ? With a fine imitation of the classic shrug of the French *fonctionnaire* he told me that that was my business. I went to Mohamedaly's. The manager told me that his brother had now been waiting ten days, trying to collect enough thalers for his ticket to Djibouti. I was willing to pay a good price for them, I said. So, remarked the manager, was his brother. Mr. Costi, the manager at Bolo-lakos's Hotel, had a good laugh when I tried to change money with him. Everyone in Diredawa wanted thalers, he said. But what must I do ? I must stay in Diredawa like everyone else, Mr. Costi suggested ; he added that it was now a very agreeable town, a military band played there twice a week in the main street.

Eventually a Czecho-Slovak was discovered who had a small cache he was willing to change against sterling ; so in great secrecy—we were liable to be gaoled for it—and at an extravagant price, I was able to buy fifty. The transaction took place in a bedroom. It was like buying cocaine.

Rain began soon after we left Diredawa and continued almost without intermission for the two days of the journey. There was a machine-gun section posted at the front of the train ; another at the rear. From Awash to Addis the line was heavily guarded. There had been sharp fighting there in the previous month. A train was derailed and sacked, two bridges destroyed and a station besieged for a day and a half. For ten days trains could not get through. The affair was inadequately reported from official sources and enormously exaggerated by rumour. Several lives were lost. When it was all over a Greek woman was discovered under the train, clutching two children, scared almost out of her wits but uninjured except for a black eye. After that Eritrean troops had been sent to ' clean up ' the villages in the vicinity. By all accounts they had done the job with relish. Now there were blackshirts and white troops camped in the mud at every station. They called out for newspapers as we passed. At one station we met a group of Italian soldiers talking to each other in English. They were volunteers from the United States who had forgotten their native language. All the white troops, both here and elsewhere, looked very fit and very bored.

The children along the line crowded round the carriages begging in their accustomed manner. But they had learned some new tricks. *Si salute romanamente.* They could all cry *Viva Duce!* Some of them could sing 'Giovanezza.' They were rewarded with handfuls of small change.

The promise of the station-master at Diredawa that another coach would be added at Awash to relieve the acute overcrowding was not fulfilled. Eventually, at sunset on the second day, we came to the end of our journey.

2

I was received two days later by the Viceroy. He lived in temporary quarters at the Emperor's New Gibbi, in the minimum of personal splendour.

Indeed it would have been impossible to be splendid in that seedy villa. The structure had suffered little during the days of pillage, but it had been robbed of most of its furniture and looked as woebegone as a bankrupt casino. The floors were stripped of their carpets and the cheap parquet was already buckled and warped ; patches of damp discoloured the paint ; here and there plaster had cracked and flaked away ; curtains had been torn down and windowpanes broken ; strands of wire protruded from walls, ceilings and cornices, where the rioters had snatched at sconces and electric fittings. (The mob were fanciful in their depredations. A Swedish doctor, who had given his whole life to the service of the Abyssinians, was shocked to encounter a Galla woman walking out of his surgery with his microscope balanced on her head.)

The Viceroy's own apartments were tolerably furnished with the few gilt chairs and imitation French tables that had been salvaged. Graziani was in his Marshal's field uniform sitting at a desk laden with official papers. The autocratic tradition persisted and he found himself, I was told, responsible for the details of every branch of the administration ; every decision, however trivial, was referred to him.

He gave me twenty minutes. I have seldom enjoyed an official audience more. His French was worse than mine, but better than my Italian. Too often when talking to minor fascists one finds a fatal love of oratory. The morning before I had been present when the German Consul-General paid a visit to the fascist headquarters. The officer-in-charge—a blackshirt political boss from Milan—had straddled before us, thrown out his chin, flashed his gold teeth and addressed his audience of half a dozen upon the resurgence of Rome, the iniquity of sanctions and the spirit of civilisation and the Caesars, in a manner carefully modelled upon that of the Duce speaking from the balcony of the Palazzo Venezia. There was no nonsense of that kind about Graziani. He was like the traditional conception of an English admiral, frank, humorous and practical. He asked where I had been, what I had seen, what I wanted to see. Whenever my requests were reasonable he gave his immediate consent. If he had to refuse anything he did so directly and gave his reasons. He did not touch on general politics or the ethics of conquest. He did not ask me to interpret English public opinion. How long had I got for my visit ? Did that time include my return journey ? He knew exactly how long it would take under existing conditions to reach any particular place, what facilities I should find for transport, what accommodation on arrival. He urged me to go South and see the line of his own advance. I said I preferred, in the limited time at my disposal, to visit the North. He immediately authorised my journey from Asmara as far as Lake Ashangi and, if I wished it, to Dessye ; I might use the military air service from Diredawa to

Massawa. He made a few caustic and well-deserved criticisms on the war-time press service in Addis Ababa. He declined to commit himself about the ultimate development of the new territory ; his immediate concern was the job in hand—pacification. Then, referring to a dossier before him : ' You were here for the Negus' coronation. Would you recognise the crown ? '

He called to his clerk, who unlocked a red plush hat-box and produced the crown of Ethiopia, recently recovered from the looters. It was not the old crown of Theodore which we used to keep in London, but the silver-gilt local product used for the coronation, about which reporters at the time had composed such extravagant fables. It had never been very beautiful or very valuable. Now it was a pathetic, commonplace thing, the cross at the top loose and hanging askew ; every stone had been prised out of it. But it was still recognisable as the ornament that had been used on that absurd occasion. It recalled the aspect of the assembled dignitaries— the Duke of Gloucester, the Prince of Udine, Marshal d'Esperey, Mr. Jacoby from U.S.A., and all the meaningless good words that had graced the day. He asked about the book I was going to write ; said he was sure he would not have time to read it, and dismissed me. I left with the impression of one of the most amiable and sensible men I had met for a long time.

3

It was clear that Asmara, not Addis, would have to be my centre for seeing the battlefields and the working of the new administration in the conquered territories. Meanwhile there was enough to keep me interested, between trains, in renewing acquaintances and observing the changes in the capital.

Addis, as has been already suggested, was never a town of outstanding amenities. At this season of this particular year it seemed preternaturally forbidding. The central square, where the Post Office, the two cinemas and the principal European shops had stood, was still as it had been left by the rioters, a heap of blackened masonry, charred timber and twisted iron. For weeks now the Dessye Road had been impassable; the railway was the sole means of communication with the outside world and this had been working to its utmost capacity to keep the city, whose population was now increased by a garrison of forty thousand troops, in flour and the bare necessaries of life. It had been impossible to import building materials and all work of reconstruction had thus been postponed until after the rains. Every available building had been taken over to provide quarters for the new civil and military population; a ring of temporary forts protected the city, where the men lived under canvas behind timber stockades and waged a ceaseless war on the floodwater which seeped in from all sides and lay everywhere in shallow pools of muck. The commissariat department were faced with a formidable task. They provided an adequate supply of essential food, but no surplus and very few luxuries. Prices, though controlled, were abnormally high ; most things were three or four times their usual price, some things ten times ; eggs, milk, butter and vegetables were very rare indeed. The private soldier's five lire a day did not go far in supplementing his rations ; he had wine once a week and lived mainly on coarse dry bread and spaghetti and meat stew. Petrol was rigidly controlled ; an occasional densely crowded bus might be seen, but the taxis, once so numerous, had disappeared from the streets. So had the natives. The crowds of white figures which formerly had filled the streets, teeming in to market, lounging and trotting and brawling from sunrise to dusk, were scattered about the countryside. They were shy of the new regulations. They did not like the new money. They had nothing to sell. Many of the tukals had been destroyed and deserted during the riots. The native population who remained were being humanely treated. Those who had got employment were well paid, but there was an ample supply of white labour for most purposes of the moment. A big school had been established where the children were fed, clothed and taught to sing patriotic songs. They were the happiest people in the city. The Italians, as everyone knows, love children and it was the most

common sight to see groups of Italian soldiers playing with small Abyssinians in a manner which
shocked the race-conscious of the German colony.

It was difficult to get information about what was
going on outside, for beyond the stockades lay a
closed country, but people who had lately come to
town reported that wherever they went in Shoa
and round Addis they found that the fields had not
been planted. It seems almost certain that during
its first year the new régime will be faced with
serious famine throughout the whole district from
Addis Ababa to Amba Alagi.

The foreign population were far from easy. They
had changed the names of the shops and cafés—
Ristorante di Bologna, Vulpa di Roma, etc.—and
made the most cordial demonstrations of loyalty,
but the authorities were gradually weeding out the
undesirables ; they had always been a shady lot and
few of them can, at heart, have felt much confidence
in their own desirable qualities. The Idots had
gone. M. Kakophilos remained. M. and Mme.
Moriatis survived but in sadly reduced circumstances.
Le Select had been completely sacked in the riots.
Moriatis inhabited a temporary shed among the
ruins and was struggling through the transition period
by selling cups of coffee to lorry drivers. He still
spoke hopefully of the chic bar, restaurant and
cinema which he would build after the rains. Meanwhile he was being cut out by the most improbable
of competitors—Mr. and Mrs. Heft. The *Deutsches*

Haus was now named ' Pensione Germanica.' My
bedroom was used for dinner and the former
dining-room was metamorphosised. A new, almost
modernistic bar ran along one side of it, served by
a white barman in a white mess-jacket with scarlet
carnation. The faithful Orgi, the only one of Heft's
servants to fight for him in the riots, collected hats
and sticks at the door. An illuminated aeroplane
propeller revolved in the ceiling and Heft in dinner
jacket and stiff shirt presided over a highly decorous
and much frequented ' dancing.' There were no
geese now in the yard to attack his elegant clientele.

There was a general sense of insecurity—un-
reasonable but infectious. The raids on the town
were futile ; the chance of a rising inside it, remote.
But all the time there was an illusion of being
besieged. The thick groves of eucalyptus which
surround Addis on all sides provided perfect cover
for attack and retreat ; no attempt had been made
to cut a defensive boulevard ; the bandits could and
frequently did advance unobserved to a few yards of
the outer defences ; more than this, the circum-
ference of the town is so large and its boundaries
so ill defined, the ground so broken with watercourses and footpaths, that they could effortlessly
penetrate the defences at twenty places. If they left
their arms behind them they could walk into the
town by the main roads unchallenged. In an attack
in July several hundred armed raiders got into the
centre of the city before they were discovered and

wiped out in one of the gulleys. A few days before
my arrival an English acquaintance of mine was
visited at his house, on a small matter of business,
by a young Abyssinian chief whom he knew to be a
bandit.   The youth said he had left his machine-gun
in the charge of his companions a mile or so outside
the town and was taking a day's holiday to see how
things were going.   He was returning that evening
to do a little shooting.   My friend said : ' You are
mad.   There are forty thousand fully equipped
troops in this town.   There are not five thousand
Abyssinian soldiers within a week's march.   Go
back to your farm. Leave your machine-gun where
it is.   Grow food for the coming year and forget
about the war.'

' Oh no, you are entirely misinformed.   The city
will be taken next week or the week after.   The
English have sent two hundred aeroplanes and they
are coming to bomb it.'   And he went back con-
fidently to his machine-gun in the woods.

We had a raid one evening during the four days
of my visit.   I had an appointment that afternoon
to visit Ras Hailu ; drove out to his house beyond
the American hospital and was politely informed
that his Highness was unable to see me ; he had
gone out to a battle.   From the tukals round
Hailu's house his soldiers were scampering about
with rifles, buckling on their cartridge belts ;
others were loading a car with ammunition cases.
The official of the Ministero Stampa, who was look-

ing after me, seemed embarrassed. It was the first I had heard of it. Later the news got about. Ras Kassa's son was attacking the aerodrome. Bombers arrived from Diredawa. It was quite a battle. They fought on for some hours and then retreated after robbing a few bodies. At dawn we were disturbed by artillery shelling the woods from the old Gibbi. All that day the European underworld went about with despondent expressions. There was to be another attack that night, in great strength, they said ; this time the natives inside would rise and massacre the garrison. Nothing happened ; not a shot was fired. But, however extravagant one knew these rumours to be, they made one restless.

I dined that night at our legation and found, when the car came for me, that the Italians had thoughtfully posted a bearded carabinieri, armed with a light machine-gun, on the seat beside the chauffeur. On the preceding afternoon the German Consul-General had given me a lift in his car. I was discomfited to find myself sitting on two hand-grenades which he always kept loose in case of emergency on the seat next to him.

Nothing could be easier but, in fact, less candid than to make political copy, as many émigrés have done, of incidents of this kind. It would be easy to write ironically about the Pax Romana and contrast the public utterances in Rome with conditions in the heart of the new Empire. It would be easy to represent the Italian conquest, as the Greek at

Djibouti had done, as a bluff which, in the general anxiety of the world, everyone in Europe was eager to accept without investigation. It is for precisely this reason that the Italians have closed the frontier to foreign journalists. I can well imagine what some of the more excitable of my former colleagues could have made of the material.

The truth, I think, is simply this. That the Italians have had a thoroughly dismal wet season. They have never for a moment been in serious danger. Lorries have been ambushed, sentries have been sniped. They do not pretend, at the moment, to effective control of more than the strategic skeleton of the country. There are vast areas which are wholly given over to marauding bands of Abyssinians. These men own no sort of allegiance to the former Shoan monarchy, or to any leader above their immediate chief. They exist in companies of anything from five thousand to a hundred. They live by pillage. They have a good supply of arms and ammunition, partly the remains of those issued to them by the Emperor, partly what they took from the armouries which he threw open to them when he fled, partly what they have captured from the Italians. At Gore itself and for an infinitesimal radius about it there was something which still claimed to be the legitimate successor to the Emperor's government ; [1] the rest of the country is a no man's

[1] Imru is now credibly reported to have fled to the Sudan.— E. W., *Oct. 9th*, 1936.

237

land where the Italians or any European protectors [1] are eagerly awaited by the population who at present are suffering hideous depredations.

This lapse into anarchy is a thing which greatly surprised those who know the country well, and is barely comprehensible to those who do not. When the Abyssinian armies broke the men did not, as might have been expected, make their way home as best they could to their own farms ; they formed into small, mutually hostile, bands. It was not merely a question of the subject tribes revolting against the Amharas—nearly everyone had expected that—but of the Amharas savagely at war among themselves. I met in Addis Ababa a European doctor who had had the unique experience of spending the whole of the war with the army of Ayula Berru. He was unconnected with any Red Cross unit. At the beginning of hostilities he had been asked by the Emperor to go North and attend this chief who was ill. He had consented on condition that he was allowed to return immediately. This was promised. He was flown to Berru's camp, where he found 15,000 men, first-class fighting material, well armed. He cured the chief but his application to return was refused. From then onwards he shared the fortunes of the army. They advanced in the highest spirits, won two sharp

[1] See the reports, unobtrusively summarised in *The Times* of September 28th, 1936, of the British Consul at Gore and the Sudan District Commissioner at Gambeila.

engagements and by December were in a strong
position to harass the Italian lines of communication,
then unduly extended and suffering from grave
difficulties. This was consistently forbidden by the
Emperor, who maintained intermittent relations
with them by wireless. The army halted and
camped on the Eritrean frontier. From that moment
desertions began in ever-increasing numbers. They
were bombed regularly but the country was full of
caves and casualties were not serious. Gas was used
but accounted for only eighteen lives.[1] The men were
bored and exasperated with a weapon to which they
could make no effective answer. In two months
the army had dwindled to 5000 men. Berru then
began his retreat. Once the army was in column
it provided an easy target. They were consistently
bombed from the air by day. At night they could
not make camp because they were being followed
and attacked at every stage of their journey by their
own deserters. They reached Gondar after a

---

[1] It is difficult to get reliable figures, but it seems that at no time
was gas or ypirite very effective as a lethal weapon. Nor was it
primarily used as such. Its value to the invading army was to
sterilise the bush along the line of advance, so that the mechanised
column could push forward rapidly without fear of ambush. It
was not used at Dessye or Harar or, as far as I know, on any town.
Great publicity was given at the time to the gas cases which came
to the hospitals for treatment. All wounds and all the effects of
war are, of course, hideous. Actually those caused by gas and ypirite
appear to have been far fewer in number and more temporary in
character than those of other weapons. In breaking the Abyssinian
morale machine-gunning from the air appears to have proved the
most effective arm.

frightful march, during which they had been on the move day and night with no provisions other than what they could find in a countryside already pillaged by their former comrades. At Gondar they found the town fortified against them by the inhabitants. They turned North again and for weeks stumbled back along the road they had come, starving, ragged, dwindling daily in number from casualties and desertions, attacked ceaselessly by both races until, some time after the Emperor's flight, Berru surrendered with a handful of men to an Italian military post. That was what was going on all over the country in April and May. In many parts things seem to have been worse. Berru was a fighter and he maintained some sort of authority over some of his men. In districts where the conservative hereditary nobles had been dispossessed and their places taken by the Emperor's nominees—semi-educated, semi-Westernised members of the patriotic party—the men were often left without a semblance of leadership, for the qualities which had enabled the new aristocracy to rise in royal favour were not those which were needed at a time of national disaster.

The collapse of the Shoan system of government and the whole illusion of national unity was so sudden and so complete that no one was prepared for it. The Italians had accomplished in six months a task which they had expected to take two years. They now found themselves faced with opportunities and responsibilities vastly greater than their ambitions at the beginning of the war. It was a triumph in Rome. It was the end of the war as far as Europe was concerned. But it was the beginning of an enormous work in Africa and of work which had to be postponed through tedious months of rain. The conquering army were enjoying few of the fruits of victory. They had still to be maintained at war strength and in war conditions. They were told that peace had been declared but they lived in constant vigilance. There was nothing to do except sit about sheltering from the rain and gaze out from the sentry posts into the dripping eucalyptus ; to go into action when it suited the temper of the marauding bands to come and shoot at them. It was a severe test of morale and they stood up to it in a way which should dispel any doubts which still survive of the character of the new Italy. By the time that these words appear in print the period of waiting will be over. The roadmakers and soldiers will have started on the second decisive campaign. Plans are already being drawn up for a new city at Addis. In a few months it will seem incredible that one drove out to dinner with a machine-gunner on the box, that one found hand-grenades in the back seat. The new régime is going to succeed. But I am glad to have seen the town at the moment of the transition.

VII

THE ROAD

I

WE were late in leaving Diredawa ; we stopped to lunch and gossip at Assab ; it was four o'clock before we landed at Massawa ; an afternoon of burning, breathless heat, far hotter than noon at Assab. We had flown at a great height in the big, three-engined Caproni bomber ; there was nothing to see in that country, nor could I have seen it from my place in the gun turret ; once or twice I climbed down to the observation pit, but found an unvarying landscape of coast, sand dune and minute, dry watercourses. Currents of icy wind drove through the machine ; we sat huddled in leather overcoats. It was an odd feeling to drop suddenly to sea-level and step out on to the blistering sand of the hottest place in the Red Sea ; an agreeable feeling for the first few seconds, a tingling all over the skin which made one shiver, succeeded almost immediately by a sense of dead oppression.

I had spent a night in Massawa on the voyage out, and did not wish to repeat the experience. The

242

aerodrome was deserted. We sat for an hour in the shade of a hangar. Then a car arrived and we were able to get a lift to headquarters. There we found a good-natured captain who was on the point of starting for the hills. He offered me a place in his car and a bed in his camp at Gura. We started at dusk.

It was the beginning of the great trunk road that climbs from Massawa to Asmara and then runs through the mountains along the line of Badoglio's advance, through Adigrat, Makale, Kworam and Dessye ; within a few weeks of the appearance of these words in print it will have reached Addis Ababa ; thence to go through the unconquered territories of the South to the Somali coast and Mogadishu. With its vast tributaries, of which Dessye is to be the point of confluence, it is at once the symbol and the supreme achievement of the Italian spirit. A main road in England is a foul and destructive thing, carrying the ravages of barbarism into a civilised land—noise, smell, abominable architecture and inglorious dangers. Here in Africa it brings order and fertility.

During the succeeding fortnight I travelled the length of it until it petered out into a rough military track South of Lake Ashangi. It is a tremendous work, broad, even, perdurable ; a monument of organised labour. It crosses some of the most formidable country in the world ; sometimes following the contours, cut in the rock face, borne on great

buttresses and ramparts of concrete and faced stone ;
continually descending into the ravines with which
the country is scored, in a multitude of delicately
graded hairpin bends ; bridging the rivers on
Roman arches and climbing again into the mountains
beyond ; sometimes running dead straight across the
plain on high stone embankments.

In all the years of external peace, with European
advice and unlimited native labour, the Shoan
Government, whose chief need and avowed aim
was the improvement of communications, had only
succeeded in making the pathetic tracks from Addis
Ababa to Dessye, and from Diredawa to Jijiga ;
there are still English Liberals who maintain that,
left to himself, the Emperor would have accomplished all that the Italians hope to do for the development of his country. The Italian road has been
built in a few months of exceptional difficulty to last
for centuries. The workmen followed literally at
the heels of the conquering army. In late summer
we sped comfortably at sixty miles an hour over the
battlefields of the early Spring. At one point we
passed the graves of seventy civilian workmen who
were surprised, unarmed, by an Abyssinian raiding
party, and butchered with every traditional atrocity.
(A monk was the leader of that enterprise.) After
the fighting came the rains, but the work went on.
While the route was still in construction, a continuous stream of transport, taking supplies to the
troops, followed as best it could. Much of the

country over which it travelled was desert, much depopulated and despoiled. There was constant difficulty in supplying the workmen with food and materials, but they worked on. And when they rested they employed their leisure in embellishing the road they had made with little gardens of saplings and wild flowers, ornamental devices of coloured pebbles, carved eagles and wolves, fasces and heads of Mussolini, inscriptions, in the Roman fashion, recording the dates and details of their passage.

2

Asmara may have been a decent enough little town before the war when it was built to accommodate a white population of 2000. Now there were 60,000 and it was hell. Dense, aimless, exclusively male, white crowds thronged the streets. Every shop, restaurant and place of entertainment, even the Cathedral, was unendurably overfull. The hotel ran Mr. Kakophilos close for the All-Africa booby prize and only failed by a short head through the superiority of the servants ; Italians do not seem to know how to wait badly. But it was a revelation to me to find that they can prepare uneatable macaroni. I occupied the same quarters as those described by Mr. Mortimer Durand in *Abyssinian Stop Press*. I can assure him that they have in no way improved ; have in fact deteriorated by reason of an invasion of fleas. In fact I was so badly bitten that when I showed the marks to Captain Franchi, of the Press Bureau, he could not believe that fleas existed in such numbers anywhere in the world and remarked sceptically " Perhaps it is your stomach." It was no fault of Franchi's, to whom were due all the amenities and none of the discomforts of my visit. He proved throughout the most thoughtful and efficient of hosts. This was all the more noble in him since my arrival came as a bitter disappointment.

The Viceroy had telegraphed to him from Addis to expect me. Like many others before him, he was deluded by my Christian name and for two days flitted between airport and railway station, meeting every possible conveyance, in a high state of amorous excitement. His friends declared that he had, with great difficulty, procured a bouquet of crimson roses. The trousered and unshaven figure which finally greeted him must have been a hideous blow, but with true Roman courtesy he betrayed nothing except cordial welcome, and it was only some days later, when we had become more intimate, that he admitted his broken hopes.

For there were only seven unattached white women among the 60,000 men of Asmara and feminine company is a primary need for Italians, the lack of which is for them one of the most severe hardships of the campaign. It is a romantic rather than a physical need ; the latter, in a rough and tumble way, has been catered for. Teutons, on the whole, welcome prolonged holidays from their womenfolk and, at home, invent clubs and sports and smoking rooms where they can escape and get together a male society. But Latins like the presence of women. The simple soldiers missed the domesticity of their cottages—the wives and daughters and grandmothers and visiting aunts and sisters-in-law ; the officers wanted to dance and meet women at dinner and gossip with them. Almost all conversations in Ethiopia reverted very quickly to the subject of women. Everyone had been envying Franchi his privileged opportunities as my guide ; there had been the keenest speculation about my age and appearance. I could not have been a keener disappointment ; nor could I have been treated with greater consideration if I had in fact been the woman they were all hoping for.

One day Franchi and I drove to Axum. We started before dawn and, as the sun came up over the crest of the mountains and the grey, watery mist that had drifted across the headlights began to clear, we saw the navvies emerging from their camps for work on the roads. We passed them all day, sometimes in gangs, working concrete mixers, sprays of hot asphalt, steam rollers : sometimes holding us up as a charge of dynamite shattered the rock ahead of us, sometimes scattered in ones and twos over a mile of road, squatting at the side breaking stones ; for the work was being done in sections and there was still places where one diverged from the new route and followed the rough military track made by the sappers. At times all three lines were visible, crossing and recrossing one another—the new highway, the temporary water-bound road of the mechanised army, and the old, precipitous, straggling mule track along which the caravans still passed.

The men were, for the most part, older than the soldiers ; sturdy, middle-aged, apparently indefatigable men (for they were still working when we repassed them at sunset with the same resolute application they had shown early in the day). Some of them were patriarchal, with long grizzled beards. They wore the clothes which they would have worn to work in Italy except for the addition of a sun helmet—in most cases rendered shapeless now by rain and wear.

It was a new thing in East Africa to see white men hard at work on simple manual labour ; the portent of a new type of conquest.

To the other imperial races it was slightly shocking. To the Abyssinians it was incomprehensible. To them the fruit of victory is leisure. They fought their wars against the neighbouring tribes, won them as the Italians had done, through superior arms and organisation, and from then onwards settled back to a life of ease. The idea of conquering a country in order to work there, of treating an empire as a place to which things must be brought, to be fertilised and cultivated and embellished instead of as a place from which things could be taken, to be denuded and depopulated ; to labour like a slave instead of sprawling idle like a master—was something wholly outside their range of thought. It is the principle of the Italian occupation.

It is something new in Africa ; something, indeed, that has not been seen anywhere outside the United States of America for two hundred years. English colonisation has always been the expansion of the ruling class. At the worst it has been the achievement of rich men trying to get richer ; at the best it has been the English upper classes practising among the simpler communities of the world the virtues of justice and forbearance and sympathy which they have inherited and for which their own busier civilisation gives less scope. It has always been an aristocratic movement and the emigrant of humble origin in his own home finds himself a man of position in the colonies, with dignity and responsibilities, a host of servants, the opportunities for expensive sport, and the obligation of a strict rule of conduct, simply by reason of his being an Englishman in an English colony. The " poor white " is a thing to be abhorred, to be pushed out of sight ; white men are only permitted to be underdogs in their own countries. But the Italian occupation of Ethiopia is the expansion of a race. It began with fighting, but it is not a military movement, like the French occupation of Morocco. It began with the annexation of potential sources of

wealth, but it is not a capitalistic movement like
the British occupation of the South African gold-
fields. It is being attended by the spread of order
and decency, education and medicine, in a dis-
graceful place, but it is not primarily a humane
movement, like the British occupation of Uganda.
It can be compared best in recent history to the great
western drive of the American peoples, the dis-
possession of the Indian tribes and the establishment
in a barren land of new pastures and cities.

Adowa was completely unscarred by war and
apparently thoroughly happy. It is a more imposing
city than anything in the South. The Tigreans
retain a sense of architecture from their ancient
civilisation. The houses are often of two stories,
built of well-fitted stone with, here and there, an
attempt at ornament over a door or window.
There are great sycamore trees and little walled
courts round the houses. The people grinned and
saluted everywhere ; the children in particular
were quite fearless and unaffectedly friendly. We
went on to Axum, which has been fully described by
more adventurous travellers in the past. We saw
the antiquities, the great monolithic styles ; the
dingy old church which is the religious centre of
the empire ; we lunched at the officers' mess in
the grounds of Ras Seyoum's Gibbi. The usual
crowd of suitors, litigants and gossips were hanging
about, as at an Abyssinian court of the old régime.

After luncheon we went out with lanterns and
explored the finely built sixth-century mausoleum
that lies half buried in the hillside. No doubt it
will soon be a tourist resort—marked with one star
in Baedeker. We were back in Asmara in time
for dinner, having comfortably accomplished in
fourteen hours what would, a year before, have
been a formidable and painful journey.

Two days later we set out on a three-day trip
along the main road (the Axum road branches West
at Asmara and will eventually lead to Gondar and
Lake Tana) through Adigrat, Makale, Amba Aradam,
Amba Alagi, Mai Cio, Lake Ashangi and Kworam—
places whose names less than a year ago we had so
often read in the bulletins and marked, with so
much curiosity, on our maps.

The approach to Makale, at dusk on the first
evening, was overpoweringly romantic after the
temporary wooden towns, reminiscent of cowboy
films, through which we had been travelling all day.
It seemed to be a place of castles—Galliano's fort
on the hills dominating the city ; a lonely, cas-
tellated stronghold of the Emperor Theodore in the
plain beyond ; and, in the centre, the palace of
Gugsa, built in baronial Gothic for Theodore by an
Italian architect. The officers' mess received us
with genial hospitality. There was no talk of
politics or of Mr. Eden, whose name unjustly but
irradicably is now fixed in every Italian mind as the
embodiment of personal spite. Instead we spoke

of the habits of the Tigreans, the adventures of the campaign, the merits and peculiarities of the native askaris and, inevitably, of women.

Next day from the hill station at Mai Cio an officer who had fought there explained the tactics of the decisive battle in the saucer of land below us ; the battle which will go down to history, quite inaccurately, as the Battle of Lake Ashangi. He was still suspicious, in spite of all I could tell him, that British artillery officers had been fighting with the Emperor that morning. The official military history of the campaign is in preparation. I will not attempt an inexpert recapitulation of what he told me. Three facts seemed chiefly to have impressed him—the skill with which the Abyssinians had by then learned to take cover from aircraft, the reckless courage of the advance of the Imperial Guard, and the fatal two days' delay when the Emperor, who was then in personal command, hung back from the attack and allowed Badoglio to get into position and bring up his artillery. After luncheon we followed the valley to Lake Ashangi ; it was there that the aeroplanes, which had played only a minor part in the battle, were able to turn the retreat into a rout.

Large herds of oxen were peaceably grazing by the lakeside in charge of a small native. He grinned and gave the fascist salute as we passed him. A few miles further on lay the straggling village of Kworam which had been the Emperor's headquarters ; from which he began the retreat which led in a few weeks to Djibouti, Jerusalem and Geneva.

And there, for the moment, the road came to an end. The men were already working between Kworam and Dessye. Soon they would be pushing out from Dessye and Addis Ababa. Now it was a perilous no man's land of bog and bandits. They are at work there at this moment, as I write. They will be at work there when these words appear, and in a few months the great metalled highway will run uninterrupted along the way where the Radical and I so painfully travelled a year before, past the hot springs where our servants mistook the bubbles for rising fish, past the camping ground where Dedjasmach Matafara entertained us to breakfast, up the immense escarpment, past Debra Birhan, where the one-eyed chief held us prisoner, to Addis, where a new city will be in growth—a real " New Flower "—to take the place of the shoddy ruins of Menelik and Tafari. And from Dessye new roads will be radiating to all points of the compass, and along the roads will pass the eagles of ancient Rome, as they came to our savage ancestors in France and Britain and Germany, bringing some rubbish and some mischief ; a good deal of vulgar talk and some sharp misfortunes for individual opponents ; but above and beyond and entirely predominating, the inestimable gifts of fine workmanship and clear judgment—the two determining qualities of the human spirit, by which alone, under God, man grows and flourishes.